# LEADERSHIP
# LEGACY MOMENTS

# LEADERSHIP
# LEGACY MOMENTS

*Visions and Values for Stewards
of Collegiate Mission*

E. Grady Bogue

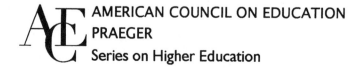

AMERICAN COUNCIL ON EDUCATION
PRAEGER
Series on Higher Education

**Library of Congress Cataloging-in-Publication Data**

Bogue, E. Grady (Ernest Grady), 1935–
    Leadership legacy moments : visions and values for stewards of collegiate mission /
  E. Grady Bogue.
      p. cm. — (ACE/Praeger series on higher education)
    Includes bibliographical references and index.
    ISBN 978-0-275-99778-6 (alk. paper)
    1. College administrators.   2. Universities and colleges—Administration.
3. Educational leadership.   I. Title.
    LB2341.B5543   2007
    378.1'616—dc22       2007022765

British Library Cataloguing in Publication Data is available.

Library of Congress Catalog Card Number: 2007022765
ISBN: 13: 978–0–275–99778–6

First published in 2007

Praeger Publishers, 88 Post Road West, Westport, CT 06881
An imprint of Greenwood Publishing Group, Inc.
www.praeger.com

Printed in the United States of America

The paper used in this book complies with the
Permanent Paper Standard issued by the National
Information Standards Organization (Z39.48–1984).

10 9 8 7 6 5 4 3 2 1

## Copyright Acknowledgments

The author and the publisher gratefully acknowledge permission for use of the following
material:

Portions of Chapter One have been adapted from a chapter entitled "An Agenda of
Common Caring: The Call for Community in Higher Education." This paper I originally
wrote for a 2002 Jossey-Bass book entitled *Creating Campus Community*, and the adaptation
from that paper is used here with permission of John Wiley and Sons.

Portions of Chapter Two have been adapted from an article I originally published under the
title "A Breakpoint Moment: Visions and Values for Trustees of Collegiate Mission" and
appearing in the Volume 30, Number 5, 2006 issue of the journal *Innovative Higher
Education*. The adaptation is used here with permission of Springer Publications.

Portions of Chapter Four have been adapted from an article I originally published under the
titled "The Art of Using Power and Authority" and appearing in the Winter 2003 issue of
the journal *Leader to Leader*. The adaptation is used here with permission of John Wiley and
Sons.

Portions of Chapter Twelve have been adapted from an article I originally published under
the title "What's All This Talk About Accountability" originally appearing the March/
April 2006 issue of *Trusteeship*. The adaptation is used here with permission of the
publisher, the Association of Governing Boards of Universities and Colleges.

To Dr. Jerry Boone, Lt. General John Bradley (USAF),
Dr. Archie Dykes, Mr. James Gardner, Mr. O. E. Philpot

Friends . . . and exemplars of all that is noble
and effective in American leadership.

# CONTENTS

# PREFACE

Those entrusted with leadership duty in any enterprise enter office and/or assume responsibility with three theories in mind: a theory of role, a theory of task, and a theory of effectiveness. The first theory guides our notion of what we are supposed to do; and the second directs our approaches to motivation, deployment of power and authority, orchestration of conflict, and style of decision. The third theory constitutes a belief model on how leadership success and effectiveness should be assessed.

These three theories may not rise to the immediate level of consciousness, but they are surely operative and may be inferred from the actions and behavior of those who lead. Watch the first impulses of newly appointed administrators, whether president/provost or dean/director, and note the priority of their attention and the manner in which they open interactions with their staff and others around them. Imperial and self-serving styles may be easily distinguished from servant and caring dispositions in short order.

These three theories interact with one another. If our theory of effectiveness is built on self-serving ambition, popularity with stakeholders, and frequent moves to ever increasing salaries and size of institution; then our theory of role is certain to be different from those who see themselves in designer and servant roles, holding the development and the performance of colleagues in trust and willing to make the long term and sustained investments required for good work in a college or university.

The work of collegiate leadership begins, then, with conceptual and theoretical ideas. Those who hope to be effective but are ignorant of good ideas are delusional—not a happy condition for those expected to hold climates of learning and curiosity in trust.

Thus, the practice of leadership is first a conceptual art form, calling on the power of ideas, but it is pre-imminently a moral art form building on our values, simply because what we carry in our heads will be driven by what's in our hearts. My observation is that ineffective leaders are more likely to experience derailment not because they are technically ignorant but because they have offended core values essential to trust, integrity, and human civility. A "good" leader is both ethically responsible and technically competent.

The art form is perfected, as with any art form, in practice and action. We may have acquired knowledge of the many sources of both persuasive and coercive power, for example, and our intent may be driven by noble motives, but what form of authority/power do we deploy in particular challenges of person, place, and policy? Is this a moment to fire a colleague or hug a colleague? Here the wisdom that comes from practicing the art comes into play.

Just as there is knowledge to be derived from study and reflection, there is knowledge to be derived from practice. Whether trial attorney, military officer, cardiac surgeon, city mayor, corporate manager, law enforcement officer, or college president—every effective leader will testify to the power of this practical knowledge. The knowledge of theory serves to explain how things work, and the knowledge of practice is designed to get things done. We have, however, a formidable challenge in codifying and communicating that practical knowledge. The interacting traffic among head, heart, and hand does not yield to easy analysis or transfer.

One of my hopes in these reflective essays on college leadership is to share what has been learned from linking ideas and values in stewardship of one of our nation's premier enterprises—our colleges and universities. Whether on the military battlefield or in the corporate boardroom, on the city council or boy/girl scout council, exemplifying competent and caring leadership in any organization is a daunting but exhilarating enterprise, and not less so in colleges and universities.

Colleges and universities are institutions of complex and tensioned mission, expected to serve simultaneously as cultural curator and cultural critic, to teach students appreciation for heritage even as we teach them to question and criticize that heritage. They are places of confusing governance arrangements in which the collegial and the bureaucratic are in action simultaneously. They are places responsive to multiple legitimate stakeholders, each having a vision of college purpose and performance accountability. They are places of continuing assault on common sense in the search for truth. They are places subject to chronic criticism, living always in the forum of public scrutiny. Understanding the nature of this special enterprise is fundamental to thoughtful leadership.

I do not know whether the leadership challenges of the early 21st century for our colleges and universities are more challenging than those faced in the founding years of our nation, in the antebellum and civil war years, in the great depression years, or the expansive years following World War II. It does seem to me, however, that we face a possible breakpoint change moment as every philosophical principle central to colleges and universities appears under critical review: tenure policies, student fees and financial aid, revenue constrictions and new revenue sources, marketplace principles in management, and increased accountability expectations.

Faced with these issues, college leaders for the coming years will need to be more than genial office holders, who present the facade but not the substance of leadership. They will need to be more than moral marshmallows and intellectual pillows, offering no resistance or edge of conviction when challenged. They will need to be more than academic cheerleaders, finding the parade so that they can get in front.

For me, there is a weary and perhaps angry sadness in watching a few but rising number of corporate executive officers taking their corporations, their colleagues and employees and their customers in harm's way. We have the unhappy public record of executives from Enron, World Comm, Tyco, and a host of other corporate executives who betrayed the trust of those who gave voice and life to their corporations, taking from them their financial and family welfare. Even more troubling are the increasing number of college presidents who seem intent on duplicating bad models from the corporate sector.

The eventual cost of duplicity in both corporate and civic leaders is paid by the people. The liability of executive duplicity certainly includes financial and performance trauma. More insidious, however, is the loss of trust in both corporate and civic life as we become cynics. Again, these are men and women who carried their organizations in harm's way, not so much because they were ignorant or technically deficient in their fields, but because they abandoned their integrity, because they were too callous or too narrow minded to see the immediate and long term consequences.

I am not one who believes that leaders should be held to a higher standard of morality, because this position suggests that others might be content with a lower standard of ethical behavior. The need for moral leadership is commanding, however, because the behavior of leaders is more visible and therefore more influential—do we not learn values more from watching than from listening—and because the results of leadership actions can affect the personal welfare and the performance of so many beyond the leader.

We have too many college presidents who, in the past, might have found sufficient status in being president or chancellor but now need to be known as the "CEO." More compelling and more troublesome are dramatically rising salaries and termination benefits for some college presidents, as though suddenly the complexity of the collegiate enterprise deserves such extraordinary financial largesse, often while their faculties labor in the financial doldrums and their staffs at poverty wage rates. How long before college presidents will expect to be driven—or need to be driven—to their offices in bullet proof limousines?

Consider the August 25, 2006 matter of the "Almanac Issue" for *The Chronicle of Higher Education*. In the Almanac Issue may be found extensive statistical portraits on the diversity and the scope of the American collegiate enterprise. For the most recent years for which data are available, we are treated to the power of the numbers: there are over 4200 publicly and privately governed institutions, 17 million students and 1.7 million faculty in four-year and two-year colleges, private giving totaling $22.0 billion, federal research spending of $22.0 billion, and total budgets over $200 billion.

Before we are informed on the grand sweep of the collegiate enterprise, however, we must endure in the opening pages of the Almanac Issue a depressing report of administrative wrongdoing. This report describes offensive executive compensation problems at the University of California, management problems of fraud and waste at public colleges in New Jersey, the indictment of the president at Texas Southern University for misuse of public funds for private purposes, the termination of the president of the Alabama Community College system for corruption in the system, and faculty votes of no confidence on Lawrence Summers, the president of Harvard and Karl Burgher of the University of Maine at Presque Isle. Other illustrations of soul erosion and absence of executive empathy among college administrators may be frequently found in weekly issues of *The Chronicle*.

I make no case that we need perfection in our college and university leaders. Save us from those brittle and sterile spirits who have never traveled paths of pain, mistake, and defeat. Bring us men and women with intellectual calluses, emotional scars, and character bruises—leaders with the understanding and conviction that flows from having contended with difficult decision options and agonizing moral calls. Bring us men and women who have lived in the trenches and engine rooms so that they have a capacity for empathy.

Just as all leaders enter their work with operative theories of role, task, and effectiveness, each will exit with a leadership legacy. The record of media coverage celebrating leadership arrivals in our college and universities, or any other organization for that matter, may be usefully contrasted with the media coverage of leadership departures. A few will leave behind the aforementioned tragic legacies of defeated spirits, corrupted organizations, and shameful ethical models. Just one such legacy is one too many.

The commanding majority will leave behind faculty and staff talents of greater promise, worthy goals achieved in concert with faculty and staff, organizations honoring and enhancing those talents, and value cultures that inspire others with curiosity, courage, and compassion.

## THE INTENDED READING AUDIENCE

This book is intended principally for those who are or will be stewards of collegiate mission and performance. First among those stewards are members of institutional and system governing boards. Board members are charged with discerning the competence and character of those who will serve as institutional and system presidents. They are charged with setting the appointment and compensation conditions of the president. They are charged with insuring the academic and fiscal integrity of their institutions/systems. Would it be terribly wrongheaded to suggest that every national report commending or criticizing American higher education should show up in board member mailboxes first?

Presidents/chancellors and other administrative staff are also premier stewards, and this book will speak most directly to these stewards of institutional health. Students, staff, and faculty are stewards. Being a steward is not about ownership. It is about responsibility. Stewards do not own the enterprise; they hold in trust. They do, however, carry a burden of performance responsibility, fiscal and academic.

There are other less formally appointed stewards whose caring and concern affect higher education. Corporate, civic, and political friends have a serious economic, cultural, and political stake in the work of our colleges and universities.

## THE ORGANIZING RATIONALE

In some ways, the book is built around a series of personal narratives, as stories and illustrations can be an effective means for communicating both ideas and values and for revealing their operative application in practice. Thus, the chapters are narratives of leadership ideas, tactics, and values at work. While the reader may engage chapters in any order and hopefully come away with good ideas, there is a logic flow in the chapters as follows.

Chapters 1 and 2 engage questions of leadership content and role, inviting the reader to consider the nature of the collegiate enterprise and the evolution of leadership role metaphors. Here we consider metaphors as a form of short hand theory, philosophic guides to action and ideas that shape working realties—elements of leadership design if you will.

Chapters 3–6 attend primarily to matters of knowledge and tactic in the leadership of colleges and universities. We first explore the different sources of knowledge: conceptual, moral, emotional, and practical. The later may at first appear a little strange. Our claim, however, is that there is a knowledge derived from the practice of any art; and we consider leadership an art form. Knowledge of and experience with the use of power and authority, the management of conflict, and the orchestration of change are central to artistic and effective leadership.

Chapters 7–10 explore important leadership values, with Chapter 7 serving as a bridging chapter that explores the power of high expectations as a motivational tactic. It also examines the counterpoint idea of remembering the darker and more destructive motives that some folks may exhibit. The good leader will extend his or her trust to colleagues. That leader will also build effective individual and institutional intelligence sources and conduct audits, orchestrating a leadership dance of optimistic affirmation and quiet suspicion. Patience and persistence are presented as seriously underrated virtues, and leadership style is presented as a primary consequence of what we believe, of open heart realties.

Finally, Chapters 11 and 12 examine questions of individual and institutional performance effectiveness. As noted in the opening to this preface, leaders walk through the front door of their assignments, having in mind a theory of role and a theory of effectiveness. These two theories will command all that follows in attitude and behavior.

The Afterword is a retrospective reflection. The book is intended to be an expression of gratitude for the enterprise that Americans are willing to support in both spirit and substance and for the privilege I've enjoyed serving that enterprise in a wide variety of administrative and teaching appointments over the last forty-two years.

It is also intended as a salute to those college educators and leaders who provided both encouragement and inspiration in my career, and some of their stories may be found in these essays. I have tried to honor their performance, integrity, and legacy over the years I have served American colleges and universities. These essays represent an attempt to tender a similar legacy to those men and women who will furnish leadership in the years to come, leaders who will hold in trust the beautiful and powerful mission of our colleges and universities.

## ACKNOWLEDGMENTS

I am indebted to the following colleagues who were kind enough to read the manuscript and furnish helpful feedback on style and substance: Dr. Russ Deaton, Dr. Kimberely Hall, Dr. Laura Jolly, Dr. Robert Kronick, Dr. William McDonald, Dr. Norma Mertz, Dr. Libby Morris, Dr. Ellen Neufeldt, and Dr. William Snyder. I also owe a debt of gratitude to these splendid graduate students who reviewed the manuscript: Shelley Ball, M.G. Bailey, James Devita, Jason McNeal, and Leigh Anne Touzeau.

# CHAPTER

# The Spirit of the Enterprise: Distinctions in Collegiate Mission, Culture, and Outcome

*. . . and the gift which the University has to offer is the old one of imagination. . . . It is a dangerous gift, which has started many a conflagration. If we are timid as to that danger, the proper course is to shut down our universities.*
—Alfred North Whitehead, *The Aims of Education*

Over a pleasant Sunday luncheon with a friend who is a corporate manager in the publications industry, the conversation drifted to thoughts on management in corporate and collegiate organizations.

"You know, Grady, in my business, the key words are efficiency and productivity. And if neither your people nor your technology is producing, you make changes. I'm not sure I see you folks in higher education willing to do that. Seems to me you folks could use a good dose of marketplace discipline."

"Well, Dan," I replied, "We know how to be efficient in education. We can and do use less expensive teachers in the form of graduate teaching assistants and adjunct faculty. We can put students in very large classes and in front of computers. Indeed, there are days when I wonder whether we should out source teaching to Wal-Mart and advertise that 'We Teach for Less.' Whether these options would yield a learning climate you would prefer for your children, given its impersonal nature, I will leave you to discern."

"Another thought that comes to me is that corporate attempts to be more efficient and productive mean very little if you have executives earning multi million dollar salaries while their employees are living on minimum wage. When you have executives ripping off their companies and their employees—as with Enron and World Comm—we are well past issues of efficiency and productivity. And if business is so efficient and productive, why did the federal government use my tax money to bail out Chrysler and the Savings and Loan Industry?"

There followed a lively albeit friendly exchange on how management is the same and how management is different in corporate and collegiate cultures. An important hope is carried in this opening narrative. It is the hope that those holding our colleges and universities in trust—students, faculty, staff, and trustees—will understand the spirit of the enterprise and discern the importance and complexity of collegiate community in our national life.

As we enter the 21st century, several leadership issues challenge the academic community—issues of enhancing diversity, utilizing technology more effectively, responding to calls for accountability, strengthening governance mechanisms, managing under revenue constraints, seeking new sources of revenue, integrating academics and athletics, and making proper response to marketplace pressures.

The latter issue is of more than passing interest, as its manifestation takes several interesting and potentially troubling forms. Some in our society, like my friend just cited, are inclined to see colleges as just another form of corporate enterprise. We are invited to view students as customers, to identify some academic equivalent of profit as an indicator of performance, to view college presidents as chief executive officers whose compensation is dramatically increasing over that of their faculties, to treat faculty as simply employees, to think of the premier mission of colleges and universities as primarily that of economic development, and to subject research outcomes to the vetting of research sponsors—which are increasingly corporate. Recent book-length treatments by Stanley Arronowitz,[1] David Kirp,[2] Derek Bok,[3] Jennifer Washburn,[4] and Katharine Lyall and Kathleen Sell[5] engage the challenges associated with the corporatization of higher education.

Some historic philosophic principles of higher education show promise of abandonment or serious revision. As colleges search for new revenue sources, for example, an obvious source may be found in student tuition. Major national reports lament the dramatic increases in tuition, even as state governments reduce their funding of public higher education with the full knowledge that tuition is a fall-back revenue source. In some ways, this operative public policy is a way of taxing without the force of law, with the less affluent in our society catching the brunt of the policy shift.

Some public colleges have begun the practice of charging differential tuition by academic program, in contrast to an earlier philosophy in which students seeking to be a poet or philosopher paid the same tuition as a student seeking to be an accountant or engineer. At least one public university, Miami University of Ohio, now charges full cost tuition. Will entire state systems become privatized, a policy option South Carolina Governor Mark Sanford placed before his state in a story carried in the December 19, 2003 issue of the *Chronicle of Higher Education*?[6] The State of Tennessee recently approved the opening of a new pharmacy school at East Tennessee State University, an academic unit that will apparently draw no state appropriations support—a private entity in a public place.

In earlier years of American higher education, policy drove finance. Now, however, it would appear that just the reverse is taking place, as we move to a future in which financial decisions produce de facto policy.

Thus, we face a possible breakpoint moment in American higher education, a moment when we pass from an era in which guiding principles are well known to an uncharted and perhaps discomforting era. It is, however, in the crucible of ideological change and conflict, in the arena of competing ideas and moral principles, in the negotiation of breakpoint moments that the vision and values of both individuals and institutions are tested and forged. Such moments are instruments of discovery and development, moments not to be feared but embraced. Collegiate leaders hold stewardship responsibility for an enterprise distinctive in mission, culture, and outcome.

## DISTINCTIONS IN MISSION

From a mission perspective, colleges and universities are expected to be both cultural curator and cultural critic, to honor heritage and to assault the limits of common sense, to hold hands with the past even as we reach for the future, to tend the commons of our national life while respecting its pluralism. We are expected to teach our students to appreciate cultural, economic, and political heritage while we simultaneously equip them in skill and motive to transform that heritage. These are not mission expectations of corporate friends such as General Motors, FEDEX, or Dell Computers. These are mission expectations that defy simplistic thought and that are guaranteed to keep higher education in the spotlight of public scrutiny and in the crucible of civic criticism.

Beyond the mission tension reflected in the previously cited mission metaphors of curator and critic, we find a range of mission expectations. Grady Bogue and Jeffrey Aper expanded the traditional tripartite mission to the following profile:

- Transmission—the teaching and learning mission
- Discovery—the research mission
- Application—the public service mission
- Conservation—the library and information services mission
- Renewal—the continuing education mission
- Evaluation—the public forum and policy analysis mission[7]

Another way to frame the multiple mission expectations of American colleges and universities is to suggest that they have:

- Economic purposes—to prepare students for meaningful work and careers
- Civic/social purposes—to encourage a caring for the commons and community
- Political purposes—to sustain democracy
- Legal purposes—to promote justice
- Personal development purposes—to nurture self discovery
- Ethical/moral purposes—to inculcate values

On this last purpose, colleges and universities are forums where students learn about value anchors in their lives. More importantly, they learn how essential, but often competing, values are maintained in tensioned balance. In a healthy democracy, for example, there is a need to balance those competing ideas and impulses that are philosophic anchors for a democracy—the balance between access and excellence, rights and responsibility, justice and mercy, diversity and community, opportunity and disciplined effort, cooperation and competition, service and profit, self-interest and self-sacrifice, tradition and innovation.

What happens without the balance? Competition is celebrated as the ideological engine that drives corporate enterprise. However, competition taken to its negative extreme may lead to a dog-eat-dog mentality in which ambition causes us to sacrifice integrity for personal profit—a moment when arrogance is ascendant. Collaboration taken to its negative extreme may lead us to seek the lowest common denominator of performance, in which mediocrity is not just tolerated but embraced. In their best expression, however, collaboration multiplies the power of intelligence, and competition makes us stand on our performance tiptoes. It's the balancing of these and other impulses that is essential in the construction of community.

Our colleges and universities constitute a system of both privilege and opportunity in which elitist and egalitarian impulses contend. It is a system in which the principle of autonomy, so essential in the pursuit of truth, is in dynamic tension with the principle of accountability, which is an antidote to professional arrogance and intellectual narrowness. Citadels of reason and persuasion, guardians of liberty and democracy, home of discovery and dissent, engines of cultural and economic development, repositories of artistic expression, instruments of curiosity and wonder—here are mission metaphors of no small complexity and consequence.

An academic community is a laboratory of discovery in which we aspire for students to appreciate the possibilities found in mistake, in error, and in serendipity moments. An academic community is a venture in human learning and association, where moral precept—ideas of justice and fairness, of human goodness and depravity, of rights and responsibility—may be factored from moments that can be both elevating and wrenching to the human spirit.

A sense of community in any setting, but especially in an educational setting, signifies the presence of what I call an agenda of common caring and grace. This agenda of common caring embraces a love for soul, for standard, and for system. There is a caring for the individuals in the community, for those whose welfare is held in trust and whose labor gives voice and meaning to a college or university. There is a caring for a standard of excellence and integrity. And there is a caring for the policy and physical systems in which men and women relate in both work and play.

## THE COMPLEXITY OF COLLEGIATE CULTURE

Thus, colleges and universities are distinguished from corporate cultures first in complexity of mission and next in culture and outcome. In the corporate sector, accents of policy and principle are on the motive of self-interest, the culture of competition, and the outcome of profit. In the collegiate sector, the accent is on the motive of seeking the truth, on the culture of dissent and argument, and on the outcomes of meaning and understanding.

There is a lively though confusing array of methods used to seek truth in colleges and universities. Scientists will want an experiment in their search for objective truth. Philosophers and mathematicians want a logical argument. Theologians search for truth in sacred texts, where revelation is respected. Lawyers want an argument as they contend for truth in adversarial forums. Sociologists employ questionnaires and interviews for yet other expressions of truth. Is truth to be discovered, revealed, or constructed? In a college or university, the answer may be "Yes" to all three. Is there an objective truth existing independent of the observer or is the observer a part of the truth construction? In a college or university, the answer may be "Yes" to both propositions. Thus, in the ideological culture of the university there is variation in how truth is defined and how truth is sought.

In an informing and provocative thought piece entitled "The Capitalist Threat," George Soros[8] reflected on philosopher Karl Popper's observation that totalitarian societies claim to be in possession of ultimate truth and that there is a need for institutions that allow those holding different and multiple views of truth to live together in peace. Colleges and universities are designed to be such places.

Soros' major theme is that marketplace ideas and capitalism are being adopted in too many areas of life, bringing under threat the values of social justice and economic stability, which thwart totalitarianism. Capitalism builds on the notion that the common good is best served by the pursuit of self interest and the discipline of competition. Soros suggests, however, that a liberal and free society may be threatened by excessive individualism and competition. Self-interest must be tempered with community interests and competition with cooperation. We will return to this theme in Chapter 8.

If marketplace models and ideology may prove confining to the pursuit of truth in our colleges and universities, so may civic models. Our nation's history in the 2000 presidential election taught civic lessons in the power of vote and majority rule. But truth is not necessarily to be found in consensus or majority vote. The religious majority may have weighed against Galileo, but Galileo had the truth. The medical majority may have weighed against Austrian physician Semmelweiss, but Semmelweiss had the truth. The military majority may have weighed against General Billy Mitchell, but General Mitchell had the truth. The political majority in the South may have weighed against Martin Luther King Jr., but Reverend King had the truth.

Carl Sagan's The Demon Haunted World[9] and Daniel Boorstin's The Discoverers[10] are informing books that depict the confining effects of superstition and a narrow religiosity. Colleges and universities constitute an organized assault not only on common sense but on the bondage of superstition. And so the birth of new truth may contradict conventional wisdom and discomfort majority belief.

The birth of new truth is never without pain. Any sustained and reflective engagement with this idea will again mark the complexity of culture in a college or university.

And what may we say about cultures of decision and authority, of governance in colleges and universities? There are many stakeholders who could claim a legitimate voice in addressing questions of higher education purpose and performance, in evaluating higher education performance: students, faculty, administrators, parents, civic friends and political officers, board members, and alumni. Thus, the often ambiguous governance processes, the concept of shared authority among this extensive range of stakeholders, and the often tedious processes of consensus decision making add to the challenge of leading in colleges and universities. It is easier to give orders than to call others to responsibility.

If the complexity of truth seeking and governance were not sufficient challenges to the leadership of the collegiate enterprise, let us consider the inner workings. Conflict and argument are integral to the work of colleges and universities. An organization whose mission embraces the unswerving search for truth, whose methods include the adversarial testing of ideas in public forum, whose spirit embraces a certain irreverence—such an organization will not find the search for community an easy one nor will leadership of such an organization be any cake walk.

As earlier noted, then, American higher education is a guarantor of democracy, a guardian of liberty, a protector of an open society because in some ways higher education is an organized and continuous argument. Thus, colleges and universities serve a critical and civilizing purpose in our society via the maintenance of argument, in serving as a forum in which contesting ideas may be evaluated in a public forum.

Here also is an enterprise often criticized for its fossilized views and processes, its reluctance and resistance to change. There is something to be said, however, for the andante majesty of higher education in its pace of change. Nurturing truth and talent is an eminently personal occupation, a work of the long term whose success is not to be found in a neat balance sheet for the current quarter or year. It is a work largely of faith and optimism.

Leading an enterprise of complex and contradictory mission and with a contentious culture is not made any easier when one thinks about the outcomes of college. Never mind that collegiate mission defies any simple model and that the culture appears to be a wild blend of community and conflict, of argument and ideological contention—a place where today's heresy becomes tomorrow's truth. There's the perplexing question of what constitutes the "product" of higher education, its outcome. What test, what metric will serve to describe an "educated" man or woman? What value may we place on the new truths and new discoveries emerging from higher education's laboratories and faculty offices? Where is the number to describe the economic and social impact of the agricultural extension service in our land grant colleges? Will institutional rankings in *U. S. News and World Report* serve as a useful collegiate outcome proxy to corporate profit?

The complexity of collegiate mission expectations previously cited predicts a complexity of outcome or product. Is an educated person one of our products? If so, colleges will be one of very few organized enterprises in which the "product" is also described as a "consumer." It is also the only organized enterprise in which the "product" contributes to the quality of its own outcome.

The definition of the cognitive skills associated with becoming an educated human being is not a small challenge and neither is the development of values and attitudes associated with moral maturity.

Research agenda are no less complex. What range of research inquiry will we support in our colleges and universities and will funding supporters want basic or applied research? Will a public and civic neglect of funding basic research mean the eventual demise of applied knowledge and progress? We don't have to apologize for military, economic, or health motives driving research so long as we keep a long term perspective on basic knowledge of how things work. Should, for example, our national government be funding a new kind of "Manhattan Project," this one designed to look at alternative energy and propulsion sources to eliminate our dependence on dwindling sources of oil and side effects of global warming? Or will we wait until the polar ice caps have melted and we are smothered in a blanket of carbon dioxide?

Single data point indicators of collegiate excellence, such as found in *U. S. News and World Report*, are singularly inadequate to capture the complexity of collegiate outcomes.

## THE UNITING FORCE OF CURIOSITY AND WONDER

Writing in a thoughtful and informing *Change* article "Saving Higher Education's Soul," Frank Newman offered this note and query:

> With growing emphasis on revenue streams, introduction of for-profit activities, large-scale corporate sponsorship of research, high presidential salaries, and other trappings of the corporate world, there is new danger that the public and its political leaders will view higher education as just another interest or industry devoid of attributes that raise its interests above those of the marketplace throng . . . It is, therefore, critical to ask what is the soul of higher education that needs to be saved?[11]

Newman's article distinguishes three "soul" dimensions, as he points to the civic mission of higher education, accents the social mobility responsibility of higher education, and highlights higher education as a home for disinterested scholarship.

Will market pressures confine and distort the search for truth in the distinctive culture and community of American colleges and universities? Will college faculty become hired hands and eager entrepreneurs rather than discoverers and custodians of truth? Will college presidents become captains of enterprise rather than erudition? Will the house of intellect become a house of merchandise, where faculty are salespeople hawking their wares to students, who are credential-hungry customers? Will the college experience become one of barter and exchange between teacher and student—knowledge and credentials for time and money—rather than a shared journey of learning? Will learning become just another consumer good?

With this complexity in mission, culture, and outcome, what provides the uniting force for the special and distinguishing character of United States higher education? We have advanced some answers to this question. American higher education is a forum of fact and faith, where some truths reside in the numbers and some in the mist, but the search for truth is a uniting aspiration. It is a lively and often contentious argument over the nature of truth. It is a museum of ideas once fresh and energizing but now quaint and outmoded. It is the home of our hope, where scholars labor to solve those problems that rob men and women of their dignity, their promise, and their joy. It is conservator of the record of our nobility and our barbarism. It is the theater of our artistic impulses.

It is a forum where civic dissent over purpose and performance may be seen as evidence that higher education is meeting its responsibility for graduating men and women with a sustaining curiosity, probing the limits of common sense and asking questions of policy performance in every field of endeavor. It is the guarantor of an open society where each citizen is both equipped and encouraged to think for himself. It is a place where all in the community—students, faculty, staff—are called to ask what brings meaning to their lives, what makes them glad to be alive. It is, above all, a place where the humanizing and illuminating forces of curiosity and wonder are celebrated.

A place for what T. E. Lawrence described as "dreamers of day."[12]

## NOTES

1. Stanley Arronwitz, *The Knowledge Factory* (Boston, MA: Beacon Press, 2000).

2. David Kirp, *Shakespeare, Einstein, and The Bottom Line: The Marketing of Higher Education* (Cambridge, MA: Harvard University Press, 2003).

3. Derek Bok, *Universities in the Marketplace* (Princeton, NJ: Princeton University Press, 2003).

4. Jennifer Washburn, *University, Inc.: The Corporate Corruption of Higher Education* (New York, NY: Basic Books, 2005).

5. Katharine Lyall and Kathleen R. Sell, *The True Genius of America at Risk* (ACE/Praeger, 2006).

6. Peter Schmidt, "Accept More State Control or Go Private," *Chronicle of Higher Education* (December 19, 2003), A24.

7. E. Grady Bogue and Jeffrey Aper, *Exploring the Heritage of American Higher Education* (Phoenix, AZ: Oryx Press, 2000).

8. George Soros, "The Capitalist Threat," *The Atlantic Monthly*, no. 279 (February,1997), 45–56.

9. Carl Sagan, *The Demon Haunted World* (New York, NY: Ballentine, 1996).

10. Daniel Boorstin, *The Discoverers* (New York, NY: Random House, 1983).

11. Frank Newman, "Saving Higher Education's Soul," *Change*, 23 (2000): Sept.–Oct., 17–23.

12. T. E. Lawrence, *Seven Pillars of Wisdom* (New York, NY: Anchor Books, 1991), 22.

# CHAPTER

# The Call to Responsibility:
# Changing Metaphors
# of Leadership Role

*The first responsibility of a leader is to define reality. The last is to say, "Thank you."*

— Max Depree, *Leadership is an Art*

*Strong presidents have died while the university, supposedly held together only by the heart-strangling pace of the chief administrator, proceeded with disturbing serenity.*

— Donald Walker, *The Effective Administrator*

After nine years of relatively flat state appropriations for salary increases during my tenure as chancellor of Louisiana State University in Shreveport, in 1989, the state legislature appropriated money to fund a 12 percent salary increase for faculty and staff. The appropriations guideline specified that problems of salary compression and equity were to be engaged in the award of raises. With regard to salary compression, those in need of attention were relatively easy to identify, senior professors having served the university over long periods of time and those in disciplines not first advantaged by the marketplace—education, liberal arts and sciences.

I asked for a meeting with my provost and deans and suggested that we invite the leadership of the faculty senate to join in fashioning a protocol to carry out the salary raise decisions. Though initially reluctant, suggesting that these matters should be their primary role, the deans eventually consented to the idea that broad based ownership and allegiance to the manner in which we awarded raises would contribute to community in the University.

A joint meeting of the provost, deans, and faculty senate leadership was then arranged in which I invited them to fashion a salary raise policy and protocol that would recognize salary compression problems, equity issues, and performance records for each faculty member. I expressed confidence that this could be done and departed the meeting with the reminder that to have 12 percent raise-money was a "lovely problem" to have.

The solution offered by the joint group I considered both thoughtful and imaginative. They computed the distance of each faculty member's current salary from the regional salary average for that faculty member's discipline and summed the amount for each of our four colleges, thus arriving at a total amount of money that should be allocated to each college for solving issues of salary compression and equity. The group then suggested that issues of performance be placed in the hands first of the department chair, with approval of the respective dean. Performance assessment would be based on the annual goal and performance portfolio developed by each faculty member and evaluated by the chair. This salary allocation protocol was unanimously approved by the Council of Deans and the faculty senate.

A couple of months later, as the fall semester opened, a delegation of assistant professors asked for a meeting with me to complain that the salary policy discriminated against them. Most of this small delegation had been with the university for long periods of service but none had completed his or her doctoral degree. Many other faculty had made the investment to complete their doctorate. As with many policy issues, this one was placed before The Administration for solution.

As an aside, when the term The Administration was used in conversation with me, I always asked who that was. Was the concern directed to me as chancellor, to one of the vice chancellors, or perhaps to a dean? And when the term The Faculty was used, it generally meant the last one or two faculty members to whom someone had talked, and I invariably asked when did The Faculty vote on the issue or matter under discussion. These queries were attempts to specify and invite responsibility on issues.

Now back to the complaint laid before me by the assistant professors. In one of the more satisfying moments in my career, I suggested to the complaining group that they had come to the wrong office. Reminding them that their own faculty colleagues of the faculty senate had voted without dissent to approve the policy, I suggested that they might want to take their case before the senate. They did. But their colleagues were not sympathetic to the complaint.

## FROM CULTURES OF BLAME TO CULTURES OF RESPONSIBILITY

Inviting colleagues to responsibility is a premier way to look at leadership role. Metaphors of leadership role and responsibility in all organizations, corporate and collegiate, have been evolving over the 20th century. Early metaphors of commander, controller, and director accented the mechanistic and structural notions of organizational life where conformance and compliance were terms central to the leadership lexicon. Leaders solved problems brought to them for resolution, made decisions for others, issued orders, and repressed or resolved conflict. Under these metaphors, those men and women who gave voice and meaning to an organization were viewed only as interchangeable parts in a network of bosses and workers.

From one perspective, this was a highly satisfying arrangement. It created a climate hospitable to our proclivity for criticizing and blaming leaders and allowed us to escape responsibility. There is an appealing simplicity to the "czar concept" of organizational life. As long as someone is in charge, all will be well. And if things are not well, then we have someone to blame. And if we get rid of that someone, all will be well again. What pastime can possibly be more satisfying than hallway and office gossip in which the various limitations, real or imagined, of the dean, the provost, or the president are most thoroughly masticated? This is a culture of blame and too often a culture of irresponsibility.

Newer metaphors for leaders are designer and moral-exemplar, coach and covenant-maker, servant and steward. A dramatic difference in leadership role is projected when one moves from the metaphor of director to designer, from controller to servant. Under newer leadership role visions, leaders ask questions instead of furnishing answers, call others to a standard of responsibility rather than encouraging their dependence, share threat and insecurity rather than shielding colleagues from conflict.

Under this vision, leaders work not so much to persuade others to follow their intent and will as to call colleagues to responsibility. Writing with considerable foresight, Mary Parker Follett advanced the value of responsibility early in the 20th century: "The best leader does not persuade men to follow his will. He shows them what is necessary for them to do in order to meet their responsibility."[1] And, she wrote, the problem with giving orders is that it robs men and women of the primal yearning to govern their own lives and deprives us of access to their intelligence and devotion.[2]

What makes the evolution of metaphors of more than passing interest is that metaphors are a shorthand way of expressing our theories. Everyone has a theory of leadership role and effectiveness, and that theory-in-use guides the manner in which we construct social realities and working climates in *both* corporate and collegiate settings. Let's examine some implications for the new metaphors of leadership: servant, exemplar, designer.

## OF PASSION AND POSITION

Leadership is not just the responsibility of those holding formal administrative office, but resides in the hearts and minds of everyone holding communities of learning in trust. Leadership flows as much from our passion as our position. Harriet Tubman, of Underground Railroad fame, and Rosa Parks, heroine of the Montgomery bus boycott saga, held no formal positions or titles; but few would argue that they were not leaders. There are quiet but influential members of our faculties whose esteem in the community is such that when they open their mouths all will pay attention. There are formal and informal sources of influence within our organizations.

Effective leaders will be loving leaders. Browsing through book indexes is not a routine activity of mine, but if one were to examine the indexes of leadership and management literature published in the first half of the 20th century, it would be difficult to find the word "love." But you certainly can find that word in newer volumes.

Effective leaders will love soul, standard, and system. They will care for and develop the promise of those entrusted to their care, and will exemplify civility in their interpersonal relationships. They will exemplify a caring for standards of both excellence and integrity and bear responsibility for the social and technical systems in which folks do their work.

When I moved into the chancellor's position at LSU Shreveport in July 1980, the first week we had to build the institutional budget, which involved recommendations on salaries. My seat was barely warm when my vice chancellor for academic affairs came to visit and advised that he was recommending salary raises for four of his five deans and then looked at me as though expecting some response. Keep in mind that I had been in office less than one week and did not know him or them.

I asked the vice chancellor whether he had arranged a personal discussion with the dean for whom he was recommending no increase and given behavioral illustration and evidence of his dissatisfaction with the outlier dean. He had not. I asked the vice chancellor whether he had advised the dean face-to-face that he was not going to recommend a raise and why. He had not. I then asked the vice chancellor whether he would like for me to treat him that way as our relationship unfolded. He said he would like to think about it. A theory of leadership role was at work in this encounter. The operative design values were those of civility, candor and compassion. I had no need to accuse the vice chancellor of thoughtless behavior. I had only to inquire and invite him to responsibility concerning the impact of his own behavior.

Beyond a concern for soul and standard, loving leaders will recognize that competent and well-intentioned colleagues may labor in flawed systems. Any college administrator who has experienced the anger, frustration, and enmity of students exposed to flawed systems of admission, registration, financial aid, parking, or academic policy understands the need for leaders to love the system, to care for and insure effectiveness and efficiency in social and technical systems. This does not mean that the administrator necessarily grabs hammer and saw to fix the problem personally but rather insures that attention is given to system performance. Concentrating on what it means to love soul, standard, and system keeps leaders from the cynical distraction of small issues and minds. It also encourages patience and persistence, two underrated qualities we will explore in a later chapter.

The concept of leader as servant was popularized by Robert Greenleaf, former AT&T executive, in a book of that same title.[3] Ordinarily, the executive does not own the organization but holds it in trust. The concept of servant means most simply that the leader looks to the welfare of others, to those within the organization, before he or she looks to the welfare of self. A metaphor complementary to that of servant is steward, and this metaphor was more fully explicated by Peter Block in his book *Stewardship*, with the descriptive and expanding subtitle "Choosing Service Over Self Interest."[4]

The metaphor of exemplar conveys the willingness to set the standard in behavior rather than just tell folks what to do. Writing in their best seller *The Leadership Challenge*, James Kouzes and Barry Posner describe this leader responsibility as "Model the Way."[5]

## LEADERSHIP AS CONCEPTUAL, MORAL, AND PERFORMING ART FORM

My closing reflection on leadership metaphors is to suggest the metaphors of artist and designer and the companion values of compassion and responsibility. Let me invite you to envision leadership as an art form. It is first a conceptual art form, based on the power of ideas. There can be no artistry, no professionalism based in ignorance. It is secondly a moral art form, because knowledge is the servant of our values. It is finally a performing art form, where reflection and action are linked and new understandings flow from the traffic between ideas and practice.

The conceptual argument for a knowledge of practice has been nicely advanced by the political scientist Lloyd Sandelands,[6] and we will expand on this concept in Chapter 3. Any practicing professional can illustrate those special knowledge insights derived from working in the trenches and from the insight gained from both reflection and action. For example, effective and artistic leaders know about power and authority and the multiple sources of authority that embrace much more than the authority of position.

An artistic athlete is not consciously recalling fundamentals of play while displaying a daring athletic move on the field or court. Nor does the artistic leader consciously recall these sources of authority when placed in a situation requiring the deployment of authority. From knowledge and previous experience, the correct option presents itself without thought. This apparent effortless action, however, would not be possible without the mastery of fundamental knowledge and skill and the presence of value conviction.

I am fond of the metaphor of the leader as designer in the sense that our knowledge, our values, and our artistry create and construct the climates in which our colleagues and others entrusted to our care do their work.[7] "The first responsibility of the leader is to define reality. The second is to say thank you." This concise vision of leadership role is found in Max Depree's *Leadership is an Art*.[8] Defining reality is another way to describe the work of leadership design.

There is perhaps a certain gentleness suggested in the newer visions and metaphors of leadership role. Servant, exemplar, designer—these metaphors do not easily accord with the earlier, full-speed-ahead, take-no-prisoners vision of role that projected machismo, take-charge, and directive styles. We would err, however, to misread leadership kindness for leadership weakness. If we are to view leadership as an art form, as is my inclination, then we adjust style to time, place, and personality. Moreover, we accept leadership responsibility to combat ignorance, to shun mediocrity, to confront arrogance, to expose duplicity, and to condemn prejudice.

In a major personnel appointment venture, we opened a national search for a vice chancellor for Academic Affairs at Louisiana State University in Shreveport, this following the retirement of the current vice chancellor after a long period of distinguished service to the university. An ad was placed in the *Chronicle of Higher Education* and all steps were taken to develop a rich field of candidates. However, an intriguing dynamic developed among the university deans who came to the conclusion that one of their colleagues should be named to the position. The method chosen to deliver on this intent was that one of the deans, a close friend of the LSU System vice president for Academic Affairs, both having earned their doctorates together, would invite the system vice president to "lean" on the chancellor in an attempt to persuade me to appoint the anointed dean.

I considered such a back-door approach out of bounds and lacking in friendly candor. So I invited the scheming dean in for a little *tete a' tete*. In that friendly but direct exchange, I explained that I had learned of the back-door venture and that should the dean exemplify such behavior at any time in the future, I would not slow down to ask for his resignation. I smiled and asked if he understood.

Though he replied that he did understand, apparently his mouth and mind were not connected. He did try the same behavior again and was relieved from duty summarily, albeit continuing in his tenured faculty appointment.

It would also be a mistake to view the call-to-responsibility vision of leadership role in some pollyanna fashion, in which the leader makes effective use of high expectations but is fearful of being directive and is unaware of dark human motives. The leader will be what Robert Kaplan called a "constructive pessimist,"[9] the meaning of this metaphor to be explored more fully in Chapter 7. We will expect the best from every man and woman, but we will keep our eyes open and our audits active! We will be capable of working in both the interrogatory and the imperative style.

Nor are we to assume that the inquire-and-inspire concept of leadership role requires some particular persona, that collegiate leaders abandon the rich authenticity of their own personality. Twenty years ago I had something to say about this, and I still like what I framed:

> I worry about expectations that wear away the beautiful edges of personality, working to make us smooth little pebbles that will rub against each other without much friction. When everything in our experience affirms the power of personality diversity, why are we so intent in wearing down those differences? What strength of soul and spirit is required to develop and maintain some vision of self? Leaders know. Francis Bacon knew when years ago he wrote: "It is a sad fate for a man to die well known to others but unknown to himself."[10]

## CONCLUSION: A SPECIAL LEADERSHIP CALLING

There are shallow leadership models holding forth in our colleges and corporations:

- Inept evangelists whose only tools are worn sermonettes and homely quotations.
- Managerial mechanics enamored of technique but empty of purpose and meaning.
- Friendly mannequins clothed in the fashion of power and status, thinly veneered in social grace but empty of conviction.
- Ethical chameleons and personality puffs having no moral compass, seeking only to be the cheerleader at the head of the majority parade.
- Limited personalities of cold brilliance but often infantile in interpersonal, emotional, and political intelligence, students of ideas but not students of influence.
- Sterile and brittle folks of small compassion and empathy because they've traveled few paths of pain, defeat, and suffering.
- Status worshipers impressed and occupied with the insignia of office, seduced by power.
- Trivia experts occupied with the tending of small things.

In lovely counterpoint to the friendly mannequin and ethical chameleon models is the artist/designer vision of leadership role with its ascendant values of compassion and responsibility. If you don't love, you will not lead! Loving is an act of caring! If we don't care for the men and women entrusted to our stewardship, if we don't care for excellence and integrity, and if we don't care for the environment and systems in which colleagues work, how will we inspire others with the elevating power of our expectations?

We can tell someone what to do—and on occasions of arrogance and duplicity we should. A greater leadership gift for those entrusted to our care is the gift of responsibility, of calling each man and woman to the far edge of his or her circle of promise and inviting them to the joy of both risk and achievement.

Collegiate leaders are premier trustees of collegiate purpose and performance and have a special leadership calling, as our colleges and universities are expected to educate leaders for every sector of our national life. The metaphors of servant and designer resonate nicely with that complexity of heritage, mission, and governance culture. These metaphors also carry theories of role and value disposition designed to enhance leadership effectiveness. A special duty and a special pleasure await the touch of loving leaders in American colleges and universities.

## NOTES

1. Mary Parker Follett, "The Essentials of Leadership," in *Mary Parker Follett: Prophet of Management*, ed. Pauline Graham (Boston, MA: Harvard Business School Press, 1996), 163–81.

2. Follett, "The Giving of Orders," 121–39.

3. Robert Greenleaf, *Servant Leadership* (New York, NY: Paulist Press, 1977).

4. Peter Block, *Stewardship* (San Franciso, CA : Berrett Kohler Publishers, 1993).

5. James Kouzes and Barry Posner, *The Leadership Challenge* (San Francisco, CA: Jossey-Bass, Publishers, 2002).

6. Lloyd Sandelands, "What Is So Practical About Theory? Lewin Revisited," *Journal for the Theory of Social Behavior*, no. 20 (2003): 235–62.

7. E. Grady Bogue, *Leadership by Design* (San Francisco, CA: Jossey Bass Publishers, 1994).

8. Max Depree, *Leadership Is an Art* (New York, NY: Doubleday, 1989).

9. Robert Kaplan, *Warrior Politics: Why Leadership Demands a Pagan Ethos* (New York, NY: Random House, 2002).

10. E. Grady Bogue, *The Enemies of Leadership* (Bloomington, IN: Phi Delta Kappa, 1985).

# CHAPTER

# A Rejected Russian Major:
# Leadership Knowledge Domains

*I have now spoken of the education of the scholar by nature, by books, and by action. It remains now to say somewhat of his duties.*
        —Ralph Waldo Emerson, *The American Scholar*

*Reason itself does not work instinctively, but requires trial, practice, and instruction in order gradually to progress from one level of insight to another.*
        —Immanuel Kant, *On History*

Some leadership scholars and practitioners lament the fact that public and private library shelves are filled with volumes on every conceivable facet of leadership, and yet they wonder what we really know. Is there a leadership personality? What do leaders do? How do we assess leadership performance? What evidence will we accept of leader effectiveness? What's the principal source of leadership derailment and failure: ignorance, duplicity, or political skullduggery? We await the next hot leadership text that may offer "practical and down-to-earth" answers for those on the firing line.

There is much written on "leadership by the numbers." There are five practices,[1] seven habits,[2] fourteen principles,[3] twenty-one laws[4] found in splendid leadership texts, and we will have more to say of these in a later chapter. In these brief reflections, I run the risk of inserting yet another number into our "leadership by the numbers" panoply of ideas in suggesting four domains of knowing essential to leadership artistry and effectiveness. First, however, I want to advance a conviction on the limits and liabilities of common sense and to commend the power of ideas. Do I reveal a lack of "common sense" to question common sense?! This seems a good place for the rarely used form of punctuation, the interrobang.

To be against common sense is an uncomfortable place to be. Actually, I make no assault on common sense, urging only an awareness of its limits. Today's common sense in any field was yesterday's heresy. It is hardly common sense that a book would have two endings, but readers may find more than one ending for Charles Dickens' classic tale *Great Expectations*. And much of modern science constitutes a serious strain on conventional wisdom and common sense (How can an electron behave like both a particle and a wave?). The "Big Bang" theory of cosmic birth leaves scientists with a notable headache, an effect without an obvious cause, though theologians have a suggestion for curing this headache. Indeed, it may be suggested that the purpose of becoming educated in any field is to learn the limits of common sense in that field and to experience the challenge of paradox.

We should be wary of leaders who assume office and responsibility armed only with sermonettes, funny stories, and common sense to guide them. For some leaders, it is common sense that conflict is a sign of pathology in our organizations. For some leaders, it is common sense that the only source of power/authority is to be found in position power and in giving orders. For some leaders, it is common sense that folks come in two kinds, those that agree with them and those without proper parentage. For some leaders, it is common sense that the marketplace provides the best and most correct ideology for all organizations in our society. For some leaders, it is common sense that the primary reality of an organization is depicted in the organizational chart.

Just a moment ago, I suggested that four forms of knowledge were needed to insure artistry and effectiveness in leadership. The art form of leadership embraces conceptual knowledge, moral knowledge, emotional knowledge, and practical knowledge. A brief word now on the essence of each and their integration.

## CONCEPTUAL KNOWLEDGE

Leadership artistry/effectiveness and leadership ignorance will not be found in common company. Some leaders disdain the need to know anything about the informing literature on leadership role, the exercise of power and authority, the anatomy of decision, the sources of motivation, the forms of organization, and the orchestration of change and conflict. An absence of curiosity about how we can utilize ideas for improvement of leadership performance must be counted a disappointing posture for collegiate leaders holding the promise of both individuals and institutions and the search for truth in trust.

In a Winter 2003 article appearing in *Leader to Leader*,[5] I profiled a half dozen sources of authority and power available to every leader at any level of responsibility; and I will visit those forms of authority in Chapter 4 of these reflections. A leader who has no conceptual grasp of these many forms of authority may display the same level of effectiveness as the carpenter who knows only the hammer and saw. The promise and performance of good people are too precious to be left to the care of leadership amateurs. There are important theoretical ideas related to leadership role, to the exercise of power, to sources of human motivation, to the management of conflict. The leader of any organization, whether collegiate or corporate, who neglects the power of these ideas runs the risk of taking both his/her organization and its people in harm's way.

## MORAL KNOWLEDGE

Head serves heart, however! Theories and concepts carried in the leader's head will serve the values and ethical dispositions carried in the leader's heart. We cannot escape the idea that too many leaders suffer not only from a poverty of ideas but from a poverty of ideals as well. In Chapter 7, I will engage the human and organizational debris flowing from "soul erosion in executive suites." And in a 1994 book, *Leadership by Design*,[6] I specifically targeted the disappointing ethical behavior of collegiate leaders. Current issues of the *Chronicle of Higher Education* continue to furnish weekly evidence of collegiate leaders abandoning their integrity. In any field of work, just one executive who has taken his or her organization in harm's way by abandoning his/her integrity is one too many. Leaders may be conceptually smart and ethically dumb. The conceptual lights are on, but ethically no one is at home. Thus it takes knowledge from our first two domains to build a foundation for leadership effectiveness.

Ethical behavior has roots in nobility, selfishness, and practicality. As I later note in Chapter 7, leaders do what is right because there is ethical principle to commend that behavior. They do what is right because they fear the reprisal of those whom they cheat of property and promise. Most importantly, they do what is right because wrongdoing and meanness pollute our economic, social, and political reservoirs—producing sour fruits of mistrust and cynicism and endangering democracy.

In a recent leadership seminar in a major American technology company, I had the opportunity to visit these ideas with a dozen senior managers and their executive. I used a scene from the movie *The Emperor's Club* to provoke discussion on the concept and centrality of civility in our organizations.

In the scene, Shedrick Bell, a wealthy and ambitious alumnus of an exclusive boy's school, repeats an act of cheating in a public, oral examination on Roman History. He had cheated on this oral examination as a young man getting ready to graduate. Some twenty years later, he has offered to give his alma mater a multi million dollar gift for a new library in exchange for restaging the public competition, with the same teacher/professor, Mr. Hundert, administering the examination questions to the three original contestants. Members of the original class and three contestants are invited to Bell's home in a setting that exudes wealth and power. During the restaging of the oral examination, held following a formal dinner, Bell is discovered to be cheating again by the teacher, who arranges for a difficult question that brings Bell to defeat.

Later in the men's rest room the two confront one another, with professor Hundert inviting Bell to consider that Bell must eventually look himself in the mirror and ask whether he has lived his life by any principle of decency and honor. Bell counters that he lives in a political and economic dog-eat-dog world where men do what they have to do to get done what they want to get done.

In a profane utterance, Bell queries Professor Hundert with "Who really gives a #@* about your principles?"

At this point in the scene, I stopped the clip and asked the managers what they thought about these two views of social and moral reality. One bright young manager volunteered this question: "Well, aren't we all just a little suspicious about whether folks working for us are entirely loyal and trustworthy, whether they will give a full day's work, whether they are really honest?"

I then asked this manager whether he worked for the executive of the company, who was sitting just to his left. "Well certainly. We all work for Chris."

"Is that how you would like for Chris to view you? As potentially untrustworthy, disloyal, and lazy?" I queried. You could see the mental and emotional gears searching for full engagement as the young manager thought about this dilemma. The exchange led to a lovely discussion on the values of civility and empathy as essential leadership equipment.

I then turned the TV/VCR back on and continued the scene from the film. Professor Hundert and Bell face each other following the sharp dialogue just cited. From a stall in the bathroom, we hear the flush of a commode in the background; and Shedrick Bell's young son walks out of the bathroom stall, having heard this exchange between Professor Hundert and his dad. What did I just say about pollution and the down sides of duplicity?

What happens to sear the conscience of leaders as they ascend in organizational responsibility? When we pick up the morning newspaper in any city, the stories of leaders in myriad organizations—corporate and collegiate, non profit and service, military and religious—it is clear that those leaders taking their organizations and their people in harm's way are doing so not because they are technically ignorant but because they have abandoned integrity.

Former national executive of the Girl Scouts of America and current chair of the Peter Drucker Foundation for Non Profit Management, Frances Hesselbein advances the conviction that "leadership is about how to be, not how to do it."[7] Effective leaders are indeed more than human skill clusters, well equipped with theoretical knowledge but devoid of moral compass.

## EMOTIONAL KNOWLEDGE

The first domain of leadership knowledge is about reasoning; and the second is about valuing. The first two domains are intimately linked to the third domain of emotional knowledge, the domain of feeling. Here enters both light and shadow in the life of leaders, the presence of anger and fear, of joy and euphoria, of shame and guilt, of persistence and discipline. This knowledge domain is about knowing and managing our emotions. Daniel Goleman's book *Emotional Intelligence* brought this knowledge domain to the forefront.[8]

An American scholar and personal friend, Parker Palmer wrote a brief but provoking little piece a few years ago entitled *Leading from Within: Reflections on Spirituality and Leadership*.[9] He noted that folks who move into leadership positions have a tendency toward extroversion, a tendency that often keeps them from going within. Leaders learn the skills to manipulate the external world, Palmer believes, but fail to take inner journeys of self-discovery.

I can speak to this journey and emotional intelligence. Patience is among the more difficult leadership virtues to acquire. I am still learning about patience. I opened my study of patience as a young musician, a student of the French horn, when I discovered that one learns to play fast by playing slow and practicing a passage over and over again as prelude to mastery. Later I enjoyed splendid musical moments as a member of the Savannah, Georgia and Memphis, Tennessee symphony orchestras.

There are moments when righteous anger carefully tended and harnessed is both a proper and effective response to arrogance and duplicity. There are other moments where management of anger keeps us from trouble we don't need. When I was a college president, I enjoyed responding to letters from ill-informed critics and arrogant attorneys. I would burn the circuits of my desk top computer to a crisp in tart and cryptic replies. Usually, I would give these draft letters to my secretary, asking that she let them cool for a couple of days and then be sent to the shredder or to her secret files, where she could write a book about me later.

Leaders who take the inner journey enter into the lovely discovery that meaning may not flow primarily from wealth, power, achievement, or winning. James Kavanaugh wrote a poem a few years ago with the title "There Are Men Too Gentle to Live Among the Wolves."[10] His poem celebrates the contribution of quiet lives and gentle personalities. And general of the army, Douglas MacArthur urged the cadets of West Point to master themselves before they sought to master others.[11] How can leaders design climates of meaning for others without having found meaning in their own lives? A central part of personal mastery is knowing and managing our emotions, the third knowledge domain.

## PRACTICAL KNOWLEDGE

I have reflected on the power of theory and the conviction that effective leaders should acquire the conceptual ideas that can inform practice. In academia, we are fond of the assertion, especially in professional education programs, that theory and practice are to be linked.

Knowledge derived from practice constitutes the fourth domain of leadership knowledge, and this domain is what makes leadership a performing art form, uniting and integrating all three of the previous knowledge domains and producing an understanding that comes from the doing. Now the essentials of the "knowledge-of-practice" domain are easy enough to understand. I may know what a wrench does, but that does not mean I know how to use it. I may know the essence of musical staffs, notes, keys, and dynamics, but that does not mean I can play the French horn.

The air force taught me the fundamentals of aerodynamics, the physics of lift and thrust. But when the flight instructor jumped out of that Cessna 172 back in 1957 and sent me into the sky on my first solo flight, I not only knew, I understood! The concepts of aerodynamics were invested with new meaning.

I learned about the authority of leverage and the authority of alliance from Saul Alinsky's book *Rules for Radicals*.[12] But when do I use these authorities as contrasted with the authority of position and competence? This practical knowledge emerges and becomes available only when we have placed these ideas in action in different settings.

When a political official placed me under pressure to engage in a policy of questionable merit and ethic in my role as a college president, I was able to bring gentle threat to bear on his political self-interest and personal welfare via the use of both leverage and alliance. The leverage flowed from the threat of placing the issue in public forum, in the sunlight; and the alliance derived from the many judges that would emerge if the issue were made public. Over time, the practical applications of authority have led me to understandings not possible in just reading management and leadership texts. There is another splendid understanding that flowed from this practice moment. If leaders are making decisions that won't stand the test of public forum, the bright light of day, there is a good chance they should be rethinking those decisions.

For the artistic craftsman, there is a knowledge of tools that comes from knowing what each tool is supposed to do, whether that be a hammer or a wrench. And then there is an enriched knowledge of the tools that comes from putting the tools to work. The knowledge of practice invests every concept with new meaning and links it to skill. There is no artistry, no effectiveness in any art form without a mastery of the fundamentals. And there is no artistry, no effectiveness in any art form, including leadership, without performance enriching knowledge of the fundamentals.

Writing in an article appearing in a 2003 issue of the *Journal for the Theory of Social Behavior*, Lloyd Sandelands observes that theory is the knowledge that explains things and practice is the knowledge that gets things done.[13] An explanation, he suggests, can be imparted; but an understanding can only be developed in action and practice. In leadership art, the numbers and the fundamentals are no longer necessarily conscious but are immersed in and support what the psychologist Csikszentmihalyi calls the "flow" of the performance.[14] Watch any performing artist in action, and it will be quickly clear that he or she is not rehearsing the numbers and repeating the fundamentals instruction book in their minds as they perform. They are moving to the lovely and practiced orchestration of ideas, values, and emotion.

Accessories of value and emotion always accompany the linking of theory and practice. Indeed the traffic flow may defy common sense. Here we go again, declaring friendly combat on common sense. The conventional idea is that we study the theory, the concepts; and then we go practice. However, folks who have worked in the bowels and engine rooms of an organization may be able to grasp the power of motivation theory and leadership role theory more quickly than had they not been there. They may appreciate and grasp the many forms and sources of authority, the importance of integrity, and the management of anger more readily than if they had not already learned from good and bad exemplars in applied settings.

As a young officer in the military and in subsequent leadership moments, I learned about giving orders and the exercise of position authority. When I entered the air force, I was sent to a year long electronics and communications school at Keesler Air Force Base in Biloxi, Mississippi. Each morning the newly minted lieutenants such as myself would march a squadron of men past the reviewing stand on the way to morning classes. I loved counting cadence, and in my very best John Wayne command voice, I would count out "Hup, two, three, four" to insure that we were all in step as we approached the parade review stand. However, each day when I gave the command "eyes right" to extend the proper military salute to the lieutenant colonel on the reviewing stand, I noticed that I was out of step with the men in the squadron.

On the Friday morning of that week, I gave the command "forward march" and looked back and saw that every man in the squadron stepped out with his right foot instead of the proper left foot. Each had a little grin on his face, as we say in rural Tennessee like a mule eating thorns; and it was obvious they hoped to teach the young lieutenant a small but not unimportant lesson in command relationships. When we got back to the barracks on Friday afternoon, I turned and faced the men with a smile on my face and said, "Okay, fellows, if you all can manage to start our morning parade on the left foot, I think I can get by without the John Wayne cadence counting." And here began a new and more effective military relationship.

I also learned how much you can gain with a well framed question rather than with an order or an accusation, of which I will say more later in these essays. How did I learn this? Well, to begin I read Ronald Heifetz's book *Leadership Without Authority*.[15]

And I practiced. Following a particularly dismal performance for one of my administrative executives testifying before a public hearing, I could have said to him, "If I live to be a hundred, it would be impossible for me to experience a performance of lower quality nor one as devoid of information, tact, and poise as you demonstrated before the hearing!" Or I could ask, "What did you think of the effectiveness and impact of your testimony before the hearing?" Here clearly is an adventure in knowledge of leadership role, values, and managing emotion. Asking questions is often an effective way to call others to responsibility, which is a central theme of Heifetz's book. And yet there are still moments in the art form that may call for a more confrontational style in which you tell folks to "Stop that!"

Reasoning, Valuing, Feeling, Applying—four knowledge domains call for attention and mastery if we aspire to be artistic and effective leaders in any organizational setting. Whether knowledge derived from practice has achieved the same status as theoretical knowledge may be open to question. Obviously, in these reflections I am arguing that there is a knowledge derived from practice and that practice is an essential contributor to leadership art. Certainly we know that experience is not a guarantor of knowledge. We may amass twenty years of experience by repeating one experience twenty times and learning very little. With a modest inclination toward curiosity and reflection, however, leaders may usefully integrate the four knowledge domains and enhance the performance promise of their people and their organizations.

## THE REJECTED RUSSIAN MAJOR: A SUMMARY

Let me see if I can tie this up with an illustrative summary. After a few years in my collegiate leadership career, I was appointed Assistant Vice President for Academic Affairs at Memphis State University, now the University of Memphis. Vice President Jerry Boone dispatched me as institutional advocate and spokesman for two new program proposals appearing on the agenda of the Tennessee Higher Education Commission, a state regulatory coordinating commission having final approval authority on all new academic programs in the state.

Upon arriving in Nashville and just before the meeting was to start, I learned that the staff intended to recommend approval of a masters degree in Urban Planning but recommend rejection of a bachelors degree in Russian. Fearing that I would return to Memphis as an unworthy academic ambassador (an emotional provocation) and face the possible wrath of my vice president, my mental wheels raced into full internal engagement. The Commission had only the authority to approve or reject new programs and had no power to terminate a program once approved, presenting a sharp decision dichotomy of approve-reject.

When the academic officer of the Commission stood to give his report and recommendation to the lay members of the Commission and to the Commission Executive Director Dr. John Folger, he cited several staff concerns with the proposal that included concern over enrollment potential and ability of the University to attract qualified faculty. He recommended rejection of the proposal and sat down. Thus was presented a conflict of interest between campus and Commission and a situation in which the Commission held the primary authority/power card.

When asked if I had any response to or comment on the staff recommendation, I stood and addressed Executive Director John Folger and commission members as follows:

"Ladies and gentlemen of the Commission, you might believe that only two options lie before you in action on our Russian proposal, and you would certainly be inclined to honor the judgment of your own staff."

"May I suggest a third option? I would recommend that you approve the Russian proposal subject to the following public record provisions. Memphis State University will agree to meet each and every one of the concerns identified by your staff within two years, with the test of our having done so to be judged by your own staff. If, at the end of the two years, we have not met the concerns to the full satisfaction of your staff, Memphis State University will agree to the immediate termination of the program; and I make that pledge on behalf of the University as a matter of public record on the agenda of today's meeting of the Commission."

Executive Director Folger leaned back in his chair and with a smile said to the nine Commissioners, "Members of the Commission. That sounds like a win-win deal that should not be overlooked. With those conditions as a matter of public record, I would commend approval of the program." And it passed.

Here was an action and applied study in the nature of decision (look for other options when you see only a decision dichotomy), the nature of conflict (look for integration and win-win options in conflict), and the nature of authority (look for ways to leverage the force of legitimate and positional authority).

And that's not all of the story. I had previously worked with Dr. Folger on other state-wide and institutional policy studies. He knew me to be a man of candor and integrity, and I would like to hope that this more personal relationship encouraged a degree of trust in my proposal. I wondered on the drive back to Memphis whether I had the authority to commit the University to the conditions of my pledge. When I reported to Vice President Boone, a mentor and life long friend, he said "Hell, Grady, I didn't really expect you to bring back both approvals . . . but glad you did nonetheless."

As a postscript, within two years I had left Memphis State University, first taking a one-year postdoctoral appointment to work with Dr. Folger as an American Council on Education Fellow in Academic Administration. In an unexpected turn of events following the end of that fellowship year, the academic officer of the Commission resigned to take another position and I was invited to take interim appointment as the academic officer, the "interim" being removed after a couple of months. This new appointment as the chief academic officer of the Commission placed me in the position of reviewing Memphis State University's compliance report on the Russian Major—which I had pledged. The University kept its Russian major.

Aristotle wrote in *The Nicomachean Ethics*[16] that we acquire virtues by exercising virtues. We become builders by building and musicians by playing. We become just by being just and courageous by being courageous. We become leaders by leading. Thinking, Valuing, Feeling, Acting—all sources of leadership knowledge.

## NOTES

1. James Kouzes and Barry Posner, *The Leadership Challenge* (San Francisco, CA: Jossey-Bass Publishers, 2002).

2. Stephen Covey, *The 7 Habits of Highly Effective People* (New York, NY: Simon and Schuster,1989).

3. W. Edwards Deeming, *Out of the Crisis* (Cambridge, MA: Massachusetts Institute of Technology,1986).

4. James Maxwell, *The 21 Irrefutable Laws of Leadership* (Nashville, TN: Thomas Nelson, 1998).

5. E. Grady Bogue, "The Art of Using Power and Authority," *Leader to Leader*, no.27, (Winter 2003): 6–9.

6. E. Grady Bogue, *Leadership by Design* (San Francisco, CA: Jossey Bass Publishers, 1994).

7. Frances Hesselbein, *Hesselbein on Leadership* (San Francisco, CA: Jossey-Bass Publishers, 2002), 3.

8. Daniel Goleman, *Emotional Intelligence* (New York, NY: Bantam Books, 1995).

9. Parker Palmer, *Leading from Within: Reflections on Spirituality and Leadership*. (Washington, D.C: The Servant Leadership School, 1990).

10. James Kavanugh, *There Are Men Too Gentle to Live Among Wolves* (Los Angeles, CA: Nash, 1970).

11. Douglas MacArthur, *Reminiscences* (New York, NY: McGraw-Hill, 1964).

12. Saul Alinsky, *Rules for Radicals* (New York, NY: Random House, 1971).

13. Lloyd Sandelands, "What Is So Practical About Theory? *Journal for the Theory of Social Behavior*, no. 20 (2003): 235–262.

14. Mihaly Csikszentmihalyi, *Flow: The Pscyhology of Optimal Experience* (New York, NY: Harper and Row, 1990).

15. Ronald Heifetz, *Leadership Without Easy Answers* (Cambridge, MA: Harvard University Press, 1994).

16. Aristotle. *The Nicomachean Ethics* (Buffalo, NY: Prometheus Books, 1987), 43.

# CHAPTER

## Boa Constrictors and Other Office Mates: The Artistic Use of Power and Authority

*To say that a leader is preoccupied with power is like saying that a tennis player is preoccupied with making shots an opponent cannot return. Of course leaders are occupied with power! The significant questions are: What means do they use to gain it? How do they exercise it? To what ends do they exercise it?*
—John Gardner, *On Leadership*

Understanding authority and using power is a leadership art form in all organizations, from the smallest of operational units to structural conglomerates of massive and complex proportion. From office managers to executive vice presidents, from sergeants and lieutenants of the platoon to generals of the armies, from patrol officer on the beat to police chief in the office, from department and division heads to chancellors in the boardroom, the thoughtful and wise use of power and authority is an essential leadership skill.

In an often-cited piece, scholars John French and Bertram Raven identified five sources of social power: reward power, coercive power, legitimate power, referent power, and expert power.[1] In a chapter entitled "Power," Mary Parker Follett defined power " . . . as simply the ability to make things happen, to be a causal agent, to initiate change."[2] In a chapter also entitled "Power," John Gardner defined power as " . . . the capacity to bring about certain intended consequences in the behavior of others."[3] Other writers offer a simplified taxonomy of power/authority as being persuasive or coercive.

Some writers make distinctions between the terms power and authority, where authority is seen as a special kind of power invested in the formality of position. Other writers move back and forth between the two terms. Whether justified or not, I tend to use the two words interchangeably to describe the leader's ability and capacity to influence behavior and events.

Among those living deep in our organizations, distanced from power towers and authority suites, there is often a tendency to say that "I don't have any power or authority." But we are rarely powerless. Poor residents of a run down and neglected neighborhood in Chicago were able to get the attention of Mayor Daley by threatening to occupy all public restroom facilities at O'Hare airport. American prisoners of war in Vietnam were isolated in their cells and stripped of conventional forms of authority. However, they developed communication among their cells in the form of a tap code that allowed them to orchestrate group activity such as prearranged singing—a subtle but not inconsequential exercise of power *and* spirit.

Consider these authority options:

- Authority of position—the ability to influence by virtue of appointment
- Authority of competence—the ability to influence by virtue of expertise
- Authority of character—the ability to influence by virtue of personal integrity
- Authority of personality and style—the ability to influence by virtue of our treating colleagues and clients with dignity and civility
- Authority of conviction—the ability to influence by virtue of commitment
- Authority of alliance—the ability to influence by virtue of shared values
- Authority of leverage—the ability to influence by virtue of threat to another's welfare and self interest
- Authority of persistence—the ability to influence by virtue of determination

The first two of these, the authorities of position and competence, are perhaps the best known. Position authority associates with formal appointment and command option, the ability to produce compliance and conformance. This is what many writers refer to as legitimate authority, an authority based on coercive and reward potential. Position authority accords nicely with a "tell and compel" notion of leadership role, a role in which leaders sit at the apex of the organizational pyramid, issue orders, and solve problems brought to them.

In a prescient essay crafted early in the 20th century and entitled "The Giving of Orders," Mary Parker Follett noted that ". . . . arbitrary command ignores one of the most fundamental facts of human nature, namely, the wish to govern one's own life."[4] The leadership art of using authority effectively comes in knowing when directive behavior is necessary to confront duplicity, to chasten arrogance, and to combat mediocrity. However, the art also comes in knowing when overly directive behavior, the raw use of directive authority, may impede initiative, diminish responsibility, and damage self respect and self reliance.

Technical expertise yields an authority of competence, an ability and a capacity to influence because of what we know and not who we know, a performance test rather than a pedigree test. Years ago I was given responsibility as director of a new information and institutional research office, and I inherited in that assignment a young man of distinctive but somewhat dubious demeanor. From my assessment and prejudice, he appeared to have several problems. First, he did not wear a tie to work and second, he had a long beard. From my narrow and initial prejudicial perspective, these matters of outward appearance projected dubious character tendencies and a careless professionalism. But the most dramatic intelligence was that he kept a pet snake, a ten foot boa constrictor, in a large tank in his office, along with two mice. Every week or so, one of the mice would disappear and make a diminishing digestive passage down the snake. The custodial crew would not enter this associate's office, and so it remained in a perpetual state of disorder. Surely, I mused, no good thing could emerge from such physical and personality chaos.

Thus, I began a work relationship with this new associate with reservoirs of private doubt and prejudicial evaluation until I made an important discovery. This associate was an absolute whiz kid with computers, able to make them perform amazing computational and processing gymnastics of the most astonishing and pleasing kind. Upon making this discovery, all my prejudicial assessments simply vanished. He could have come to work in his underwear, worn a beard to the floor and kept a pet tiger in his office for all I cared. We made a pleasant but productive odd couple. He in his T shirt, cutoff jeans, and sandals and me in my blue blazer, button down oxford shirt, dress chino pants, and tassel loafers. But we made music together in that research office. The leadership accent was on performance and not pedigree, always a healthy basis for the exercise of authority in any organization.

Forms and sources of authority are connected, are they not? We earn the right and ability to influence by virtue of our integrity—knowing what is right, speaking what is right, and doing what is right. But we can damage the authorities of position and competence if we take our clients and our organizations in harm's way by violating trust and sacrificing credibility in acts of leadership duplicity. The importance and cultivation of credibility are carried in a 1993 book *Credibility* by James Kouzes and Barry Posner. One of their observations is that "The qualities of being honest, inspiring, and competent compose what communications researchers refer to as source credibility."[5] These are also sources for the credibility of authority, and a collegiate leader who abandons integrity is certain to damage his or her authority base.

We can also damage leadership authority if we are empty of interpersonal intelligence, demeaning and degrading our colleagues. As earlier noted, leaders can embezzle financial resources from their organizations. They can also embezzle dignity and civility from their colleagues. One would like to believe that those serving at the executive level in any organization would possess sufficient sophistication to appreciate the constructive power of civility and the destructive power of degradation in relationships with colleagues. Among all organizations—whether corporate, governmental, or educational—one might expect that colleges and universities would be cathedrals of civil behavior. Alas, it is not always so.

A newly appointed university president early exhibited the habit of responding to honest but dissenting colleagues in profane outbursts and found it surprising that these colleagues no longer felt like members of the team, a college executive whose behavior exemplified a modest social and interpersonal intelligence.

The world view of this executive reflected an evaluative taxonomy earlier described of dividing the world into those who agreed with him and those without proper parentage. In short order, he deprived himself of both their intelligence and allegiance and what he might have learned from them about the health and performance of the university. An executive appointment initially well hailed in the media ended in derailment and early departure.

In this case, his Ph.D. from a prestigious university apparently did not endow this educational executive with interpersonal intelligence or the ability to manage his own anger. Leadership character and credibility enhance the authority of position and competence. Character flaws and credibility fissures can damage authority!

Consider now the power of one and the power of many. One person with courage confronting the authority of an ill-informed, insensitive, or infantile person holding formal or positional power may bring a change in perspective, policy, or performance. One courageous soul confronting the massive armor of organizational momentum may sway the day. The authority of conviction is to be found in linking courage and commitment and, paraphrasing Emerson, in keeping with perfect sweetness the independence of solitude amidst the crowd.[6] The pages of biography sing to the power of individual conviction and courage. There is a lovely novel, *The Power of One*, by Bruce Courtney that celebrates this idea.[7]

Many linked in heart and hand confronting formal authority is also a potent source of authority. Cultivating alliances and nurturing personal contact are political acts. If the authority of competence resides in what we know and not who we know, the authority of alliance does reside in who we know, and in finding common cause with them. Rosa Parks and Harriet Tubman exercised the power of one. Martin Luther King built great alliances of kindred souls, all committed to human dignity and determined to get the nation's attention and action on civil rights.

The authority of leverage is a close and complementary companion to the authority of alliance. A commanding and classic treatment, at least in my mind, for those interested in the authority of alliance and leverage is Saul Alinsky's 1971 *Rules for Radicals*.[8] Here can be found wonderfully entertaining stories about power derived from gentle threat to another's self interest and welfare. Alinsky is fun to read, but perhaps not so much fun to experience if you were on the receiving end of his tactics.

Alinsky tells the story of folks in Rochester trying to get the attention of the mayor and city government concerning deteriorating conditions in their neighborhoods and employment issues, all to no avail. The Old Testament book of Proverbs suggest that the "poor use entreaties." Having tried that approach without success, they invited Alinksy over for consultation. Alinksy's rules for radicals are that you act within resources available and that you stay within the law.

Alinsky suggested that neighborhood residents buy a large block of tickets to the next concert of the Rochester Symphony and that all concert goers participate in a generous dinner of baked beans before the concert.

The morning newspaper would report that it was over before the first movement, and the story would not be referring to symphonic movement. As Alinsky wryly noted, there was no city ordinance against passing gas in a symphony concert! This attention-getting social act was entirely legal, unless one counted the act as disturbing the peace.

There is power to be found in the courage of our solitude. There is power to be found in alliance with others in "common cause." And there is power to be found in the application of leverage to bring self interests under threat.

There is a time and place for legitimate and formal authority, and a time and place for softer forms of authority and power that may be expressed by competence and character. There is a time for firmness and a time for gentleness, a time for solitude and a time for alliance. And then there are times for what I call "guerilla goodness," for the use of leverage. The authority of leverage is available to those serving in the engine room as well as the executive suite.

Stalwart conviction, dogged determination, and steadfast persistence exemplified over the long run may be among the most under-estimated qualities of effective leadership—and certainly a source of leader power. There is in Nashville, Tennessee a multi million dollar commercial shopping and business center that is among the largest and most successful in the nation. The highly visible success of this enterprise masks the hidden story of the developer who made more than 200 presentations to potential investors over an extended period of time before he finally attracted an investor to get started.

Biography is a rich source of both inspiration and information on leadership. As an illustrative aside, students of leadership can find in Christopher Hibbert's *The Virgin Queen*, a biography of Queen Elizabeth, the story of a leader exercising the earlier cited forms of authority in a fascinating climate of political, economic, military, and religious complexity; exemplifying over a 40-year reign the authority of determination and persistence.[9]

This closing story centers on two forms of authority in contention. Within a few weeks of my taking appointment as Interim Chancellor of Louisiana State University and A&M College in Baton Rouge, a knotty tenure and promotion problem was placed on my desk. A professor in an Arts and Sciences academic department had been denied tenure and promotion in the year previous but had reapplied for the current year. A contentious faculty had moved the recommendation forward in a close, split vote after refusing to recommend him the previous year. The dean of the college and the provost did not recommend tenure/ promotion and sent the papers forward for my recommendation and transmittal to the LSU board, where such personnel actions were usually a formality of board action. The faculty member in question asked to visit with me, asking whether I would be recommending him for tenure and promotion.

Now I had no knowledge of this professor's academic specialty and I was loath to overturn the recommendation of the dean and provost. Moreover, there were other elements in the file that were troubling to me. This professor had failed to gain tenure and promotion in a previous appointment at a comprehensive state university before being appointed at LSU. I should say as well that the professor had appealed the campus decision to the grievance committee of the faculty senate, but the appeal was rejected.

Upon hearing my affirmation of the dean's and provost's recommendation, the professor referred to me as a coward, as a mere office holder without courage. As he departed my office he turned and asked whether that was my tractor parked in the chancellor's parking place just outside. His hasty exit fortunately negated any reply from me. I forwarded the file to the LSU Board Academic Affairs Committee.

A few days later, the provost and dean asked for an urgent meeting with me and reported they heard that the Chairman of the Board Academic Affairs Committee was going to recommend arbitration of the matter. The chairman was a well known and highly regarded defense attorney in the state. The dean and provost asked if I would consent to arbitration, and I indicated that I did not plan to do so.

On the day of the Committee meeting, the board members were seated at an elevated dais at the head of the room. In an arrangement similar to a court room, seating for the system chancellors was provided in a row just across a chancel rail, which separated them from the board and the spaces for recording secretaries and the board attorney staff. In back of the chancellor's table, there were theatre seats for the public and observers. At the dais were seated the chairman and five other members of the committee. I occupied the chancellor's seat for the LSU-Baton Rouge Chancellor and behind me sat the Provost and Dean. Just down the way sat the petitioning professor . . . and his attorney, lending a legal chill and promise to the hearing. In the rear row of the public spaces was seated the professor's fiancé, a woman well known and regarded in Baton Rouge social and economic circles.

The committee chair opened the meeting with these remarks: "Chancellor Bogue, the committee has reviewed the file under appeal and concludes that we have a lively difference of opinion on the question of whether Professor X should be tenured and promoted. When confronted with what appears to be intractable differences of opinion, those of us in the legal profession are inclined to recommend arbitration."

At this point, the chairman began nodding his head in an affirming fashion in my direction and inquired as to whether I would consent to arbitration. I rose to respond and while shaking my head in negative manner I replied that "No, Mr. Chairman, we do not consent to arbitration. You are absolutely correct in your assessment. The professor believes that he is qualified for tenure and promotion to Associate Professor at Louisiana State University, and we do not. He has been accorded the same decision review and processes accorded hundreds of other professors prior to him and that you have entrusted to campus judgment of quality and readiness. He has also had the benefit of campus appeal before his faculty senate colleagues, who rejected his appeal."

I continued, "The board certainly has the authority to move this matter to arbitration and we are respectful of that authority. You asked, however, whether we would consent to that recommendation. Sir, we do not commend and do not consent to arbitration."

As the chairman called the matter to a vote, a surprising outcome emerged.

The remaining committee members voted against the chairman and sustained the decision action of the campus! The rarity of this outcome was all the more notable because the committee chairman was, as earlier noted, not only a widely respected attorney but a well respected member of the board who had the reputation for fashioning compromises on many conflicting policy matters.

In an off-line follow-up, that same day a luncheon was held on campus in which I was in company of the committee chairman. With the permission of LSU System President Martin Woodin, in my first year as the new chancellor of LSUS, I drove to the home or place of business of each of the eighteen LSU board members so that I could get to know them more personally. And I had done so with the committee chair. As we walked into the luncheon, I put my arm around him and said "You know that today's exchange was not the easiest thing I've had to do as chancellor."

He turned with a mischievous grin on his face and said "Oh hell, don't worry about it. You did what you should have done." I had a fleeting impression that the chairman might have been playing to the audience on that day, responding to social pressure by members of Baton Rouge high society, who might have been encouraged by the professor's fiancé.

Here we had a confrontation between the authority of position and the authority of conviction, with each of the actors, myself and the chairman, responding to our perception of our responsibility. All authority is eventually lodged in the consent of the governed, as others have only the authority we give them. To avoid pain to themselves and those they love, folks may be coerced in their behavior in the short run, but you cannot coerce ideas of the mind and convictions of the heart. The artistic employment of power/authority for noble cause and purpose is worthy of study by every leader, if we hope to call others to both technical and moral excellence. If knowledge *is* power, then knowledge of power is fundamental to leader artistry and effectiveness.

## NOTES

1. John R. P. French Jr. and Bertram Raven, "The Bases of Social Power," in *Studies of Social Power*, ed. Corwin Cartwright (Ann Arbor, MI: Institute for Social Research, University of Michigan, 1959).

2. Mary Parker Follett, "Power," in *Mary Parker Follett: Prophet of Management*, ed. Pauline Graham, 101 (Boston, MA: Harvard Business School Press, 1996).

3. John Gardner, *On Leadership* (New York, NY: The Free Press, 1990).

4. Follett, "The Giving of Orders," 125.

5. James Kouzes and Barry Posner, *Credibility* (San Franciso, CA: Jossey-Bass Publishers, 1993).

6. Ralph Waldo Emerson, "Self Reliance," *The Complete Writings of Ralph Waldo Emerson*, Vol. 1 (New York, NY: Morrow, 1929).

7. Bruce Courtney, *The Power of One* (New York, NY: Random House, 1989).

8. Saul Alinsky, *Rules for Radicals* (New York, NY: Random House, 1971).

9. Christopher Hibbert, *The Virgin Queen* (Reading, MA: Perseus Books, 1991).

# CHAPTER 5

## Political Ping Pong:
## The Constructive Uses of Conflict

*To confront means to come face to face—literally to put our brows together. When we confront, we come to the end of our territory and stand at the border that separates us. To confront is to find the existential frontier, to go nose to nose with the outside world.*

—Brian Muldoon, *Confronting Conflict*

There's a tongue-in-check definition of political liberalism and political conservatism that goes like this. A liberal is someone who sees a person drowning fifty feet from shore, throws the drowning person seventy-five feet of rope but promptly lets go of his own end. A conservative is someone who sees a person drowning fifty feet from shore, throws the drowning person twenty-five feet of rope and expects the drowning person to swim the twenty-five foot gap. Collegiate leaders can not and should not ignore the goals and ideology of political leaders but must often walk a delicate balance line in those relationships. This is a story of walking the line. First, however, a preface on leadership and politics.

### POLITICS AS THE STUDY OF INFLUENCE

In my teaching, I often find that students' views of politics are seriously limited and frequently confined by views of politics as what takes place in smoked filled, wheel and deal, and shadowy conversations. Here are to be found mostly men smoking large and offensive green cigars, foregoing personal integrity to bring home political bacon to their own constituents while financially feathering their own nests. Our morning papers carry sufficient stories to suggest that this can be one reality, but it is not the only reality.

There is no need to treat in this discussion myriad failings of our political system that may be assigned to problems associated with term limits, personal duplicity, arrogance in office holders, and the seduction of power.

Another view, more helpful I think, is to see politics as the study of influence. Writing in their informing and widely read and cited book *Reframing Organizations*, Lee Bolman and Terrence Deal[1] suggest that there are four frames, four realities, four truths to most all organizations. The first "frame" is the Structural Frame. One reality of an organization may be found in the organizational chart and the authority and communication channels depicted there. Organizations exist to achieve a mission. One discerns a basic reality of an organization, then, by consulting its mission statement, organizational chart, and policy manual.

A second "frame" proposed by Bolman and Deal is the Human Relations frame in which they point out that organizational reality is more than charts and position descriptions. The men and women who give voice and meaning to our organizations bring their needs, their dreams and aspirations, their pains and disappointments, and their social relationships to work everyday. To ignore the interactions of organizational needs and personal needs is to diminish effectiveness of both institutions and individuals.

For the moment, I jump to the fourth frame and then return to the third, which is the focus of these reflections. The fourth "frame" is the Symbolic Frame in which culture looms large as a reality. Culture is that amalgamation of policy and physical arrangements, of celebrations and stories, of values and heritage that marks the distinction of an organization. Culture is palatable and influential in the life of any organization, defining the unspoken but driving assumptions. "That's not the way we do business around here" is a frequent clue to culture. Cultures may be patriarchal or participative, formal or informal. Architecture and physical appearance, dress codes and behavior codes further mark the culture of an organization. Leaders may build on and affirm culture, create new culture, or challenge culture. Cultures may be healthy and constructive or they may offer features of what Gareth Morgan calls psychic prisons.[2]

For these reflections, however, it is Bolman and Deal's third "frame," the Political Frame, that is of keen interest. The political frame injects the realities of conflict and authority. Conflict over ends and means, purpose and procedure is seen as a reality not to be ignored or shunned but to be engaged. Perhaps one of the greatest sources of conflict within an organization and with its external system is conflict over resources, their acquisition and allocation.

As stated in Chapter 4, I am fond of the idea that authority is the ability to influence events, and politics is the cultivation of influence. The cultivation and projection of influence involves the careful study and use of leverage and alliance. Here we see again the intersection of ideas that make leadership an art form. For me, a second dimension of politics is the act of being personal, of being face to face rather than interacting via memos and email. Having noted the importance of collegiate leaders being politically astute, let me move now to the events at hand.

## DECLINING OIL PRICES AND STATE BUDGETS

In 1982, oil prices plummeted from something over $40 a barrel to less than $20. In today's volatile international climate of oil prices, this would be close to a "ho hum" event. When this decline happened in 1982, however, the Louisiana State budget took a serious hit; and all state agencies, including higher education, waited for the bad news.

Republican Governor Dave Treen announced projected budget cuts for all agencies, and the proposed cuts included higher education. The Baton Rouge *Morning Advocate* newspaper placed calls to selected college chancellors and presidents around the state to get their reaction. I was correctly quoted as saying that we appreciated the fiscal pressures faced by the governor and that we would do our best to support his efforts to manage the state budget crisis.

When the story came out in the paper in Baton Rouge the next morning, I received a phone call from Shelley Beychock, the chair of the Louisiana State University Board of Supervisors. Shelley indicated that he was calling a special meeting of the Board of Supervisors to request that the governor exempt higher education from the proposed cuts. He further suggested that if I repeated at the board meeting what I had said in the paper, this would do little to support his attempt to get board action as cited. "If called upon by the board to comment on the proposed cuts," I said to Shelley, "I will just lay the facts on the table and indicate what steps we would take in our budget at LSU Shreveport to accommodate the cuts." Here I would like to note that Shelley was the former chairman of the state's Democratic Party.

At the called board meeting, each of the LSU campus chancellors was asked to comment on the effect of the proposed cuts. Comments were filled with proportions of emotion, exaggeration, and fact. Some chancellors suggested that this was the worst fiscal disaster to befall higher education in the past century (apparently ignoring the years of the Great Depression) while others editorialized in other ways. When my time came, I stood up and reported that we would freeze all travel, all equipment and library acquisitions, and all vacant positions to meet the budget cut requirement; and I sat down.

In an interesting turn of events, LSU board members voted against the chairman's proposal to exempt LSU campuses from the cut. This action will play an important role in later events back in Shreveport.

Just a few short months later, I arose in cheerful mood one morning only to be arrested by a story in the *Shreveport Times* that Governor Treen had indicated in a speech before the Chamber of Commerce in Natchitoches that he planned to relieve Northwestern University from some of its budget cuts. I was furious. I arrived at my office in a dark funk and asked my director of public relations, a former editorial page editor of the *Shreveport Times*, to come for a visit. She had seen the story in the morning paper. I told her that if a reporter from the *Shreveport Times* called to get my reaction to the governor's announcement, I would not be disappointed. She indicated that she thought she could probably arrange such a call.

Meanwhile, I prepared a brief press release that said something to this effect. I was disappointed to learn that the governor had proposed to relieve Northwestern University of some of its budget cuts but no other university was to be relieved. I was able to come to only one of two conclusions. Either Northwestern University was suffering severe management problems that were not yet public, or the LSU Board had made a mistake in not asking for LSU campuses to be exempt. I then placed a quick early morning call to Dalton Woods, owner of his own oil company, a member of the LSU Board of Supervisors, and a Golden Eagle Republican, a designation reflecting his active participation in and financial support of Republican Party candidates and policies.

I met Dalton for lunch and shared with him the prepared press release and asked what he thought. His advice was to go ahead and release the statement, that candor was the order of the day. So when the reporter from the *Shreveport Times* showed up at the office that afternoon, I gave her the statement. The front page, bottom fold of the *Shreveport Times* the next morning carried the headline "Bogue Questions Governor," with my release following.

There are two trailing events to this story. At the LSU Board of Supervisors meeting previously cited, I had been given direction by a Democrat, Board Chair Shelley Beychock. Now I was about to receive attention from a Republican, board Vice Chair John Cade. John had been chairman of the Louisiana Republican Party. As I entered the meeting room for the next meeting of the LSU Board of Supervisors held in Eunice, on the campus of Louisiana State University-Eunice, I noticed from across the room that Vice Chair Cade was beckoning across the room to me.

On the way across the room, I linked arms with Shreveport board member Dalton Woods and asked if he might wander over for the conversation with John Cade, and he did. John opened the conversation by suggesting that perhaps I had hung Governor Treen out with my comments on the front page of the *Shreveport Times*.

I never had to say one word. Dalton jumped into the conversational fray in my defense. "John, I think you've forgotten a couple of things here. First, Grady was one of few chancellors quoted in the Baton Rouge *Morning Advocate* saying that he and his campus would do all possible to support Governor Treen in dealing with the state budget crisis. Second, you seem to have forgotten that the LSU Board did not ask the governor to exempt LSU campuses from the cuts. When the governor announced that he would exempt Northwestern from some of their cut, he made Grady look ineffective before his faculty, who had every reason to ask why LSU Shreveport should not be exempt from the cuts. And I'm still thinking about whether Dave made the LSU Board look a little timid in that we did not ask for exemptions. So you leave Grady alone!" With this pleasant advocacy, I survived the game of political ping pong from board members.

Just a few short weeks later, a dinner was given by the LSU Agricultural

Service in Shreveport, with Governor Treen as featured speaker, and I was one among many civic leaders invited to the dinner. As I sat down at my table, the governor's executive aide came up and whispered in my ear that the governor would like a word with me after the dinner. The steak and baked potato were good, but I can't say that my digestive system was in top order as I awaited the conversation with the governor.

The governor, however, was in reasonably pleasant demeanor. "Grady," he opened, "Seems like we've had a little difference in perspective, and I regret I didn't have a chance to call you and perhaps some others before the speech I gave in Natchitoches exempting Northwestern University from some of their cuts. Actually, you were right in your public comments in the paper; they are experiencing some serious management difficulties."

I responded, "Governor, you'll remember that I tried to be supportive of the difficult leadership situation you faced as I was quoted in the Baton Rouge *Morning Advocate*. When you exempted Northwestern, however, you made me look ineffective in front of my own faculty and community, who were justified in asking why LSU Shreveport was not exempted. My response in the *Shreveport Times* story was in partial response to the awkwardness I was experiencing."

"Well, I can understand your position and mine, and we will make it through this difficult year. I will remember your supportive response," the governor replied.

"Governor, I have one other question to ask," I said. "Shortly, you are going to have on your desk a capital request to build a new administrative building on the LSUS campus. You'll remember I took you on a tour recently, showing that our administrative offices were located in the Science Building where we have no fire and security protection, for example, for our student records. The capital project is coming to you with approval of House and Senate. Will you sign that construction project?"

The governor began his exit from the dinner and looking back said "Don't worry about it. You'll get your building." And we did, with a ground breaking in 1986.

## CONSTRUCTIVE USES OF CONFLICT

We opened this reflection with a commentary on Bolman and Deal's book suggesting that we will have an improved grasp of organizational behavior and enhanced leadership performance if we view organizations through four frames, each of these frames offering a truth about the functioning of organizations. And we pointed to the Political Frame as the one most central to this reflection. An important concept in the political frame is the management of conflict, and so I would like to explore that theme briefly.

On any given day, the possible sources for conflict in any organization, and especially in colleges and universities, are multiple: conflict of role, of personality, of status, of policy and ideology, of resource allocation, of style and value. Unfortunately, there are conventional assumptions often held about the nature of conflict, and even highly educated collegiate leaders can hold to some of these assumptions. They include the ideas that conflict is a sign of individual or organizational pathology, that conflict requires a winner and a loser, that conflict is a sign of disloyalty, and that conflict is destructive. Metaphors used to describe conflict are more apt to be combative than positive. Conflict is a fight, a struggle, a war, a trial.

The most frequent and negative outcome of such conventional and limited assumptions is that leaders can treat dissenters as their enemies and will demonize opposition, both acts effectively denying them access to truth that may come via honest dissent within staff and colleagues. Writing almost a century ago, however, a prescient Mary Parker Follett[3] invited leaders and managers to view conflict simply as a difference and to look for win-win or integrated solutions to those differences.

Along with leaders in other organizations, leaders of collegiate organizations have at least three conflict management responsibilities. These are to prevent unnecessary conflict, to resolve conflict, and to create conflict. While the last option may sound a little strange to some holding leadership duty, we hope to make clear what the role responsibility of creating conflict means in a moment.

One of the more powerful means of preventing unnecessary conflict is to orchestrate a set of core values that permeates an entire organization. When I served as chancellor of LSU Shreveport, the faculty and staff committed themselves to a single but very powerful value commitment, which I call "the dignity test." Our mission statement carried this commitment: "We will treat our students and our colleagues with dignity, rendering instructional and administrative service marked by courtesy and competence." The simplicity of that value commitment became the benchmark by which we were able to measure the quality of our care and treatment in a wide range of both teaching and administrative circumstances.

A three hundred pound truck driver showed up in my office one day, unannounced and without appointment. He had taken an evening economics course, made an "F" instead of what he thought would be at least a "C." He dutifully made an appointment to come and see the instructor, who kept him waiting for thirty minutes while she had coffee with colleagues and could not find his examinations or give any explanation for the grade. This student computed the most direct path to my office and did not consult the student grievance process. I invited the provost, the dean of the College of Business and the chair of the Economics Department to come over and hear this student's report and then asked the three of them whether they felt we had met "the dignity test" with this student. This situation had a happy outcome and it was my pleasure to congratulate this truck driver at our baccalaureate commencement some two years later.

In the reconciliation of conflict, collegiate leaders have access to the same range of soft to hard, persuasive to coercive tactics available to other leaders. There are the alternative dispute resolution tactics of integration, mediation, negotiation, and arbitration. Integration, the search for win-win options, is perhaps the most neglected of these. This will not be surprising if your management reality embraces the conventional assumption that conflicts require a winner and a loser.

Mediation is a good way to displace heat and aggressiveness, while guaranteeing contending parties the retention of decision autonomy and responsibility for managing their conflict. If mediation fails, arbitration may prove helpful but can lodge decision responsibility in a third party. And if the softer tactics fail, then there are power and coercive options of litigation and court action. The thoughtful collegiate administrator will invest heavily in integration as a conflict management tool and in internal grievance processes that may provide for either mediation or arbitration; because once a conflict moves to the courts, lawyers will make money and the contending parties will spend money, usually in generous sums on both counts.

Finally, this note about leaders creating conflict. My mail frequently contains publicity brochures on new books centered on the theme of conflict. Most of those deal with the management of conflict, and I don't think I've ever seen a title that touches the possibility that leaders should create conflict. We are more accustomed to seeing leaders as organizational firemen, racing to points of crisis and conflict with water buckets and fire hoses. To think of leaders as incendiary agents, as it were, is not immediately comfortable or friendly to common sense. For collegiate leaders, however, this should not seem so strange because as we noted in Chapter 1, colleges are crucibles of dissent and forums of contending ideas where conflict is an essential instrument of apprehending truth.

From a constructive and positive perspective, then, conflict is a process of testing our ideas and beliefs and for awakening creative impulses. Awaiting discovery within Kahlil Gibran's beautiful little book *Sand and Foam* is the line "It is only when you are pursued that you become swift."[4] Not only is conflict an instrument for testing ideas and beliefs, it is a means for developing identity and self understanding. Consider this line from Brian Muldoon, whose work we cited at the beginning of this chapter: "There are times when we benefit enormously from the struggle against opposition. We become stronger and more uniquely defined as a result of the resistance provided by the adversary. Confrontation brings out the best in us. In the course of the contest, we discover and reveal our nascent character. Conflict is the crucible in which the soul is tried, tempered, and transformed."[5]

Abraham Maslow affirms the constructive nature of conflict with this note: "Conflict itself is, of course, a sign of relative health as you would know if you ever met really apathetic people, really hopeless people, people who have given up hoping, striving, and coping."[6]

As noted elsewhere in these essay reflections, I am not overly fond of leadership by the numbers—even though there are important and informing truths carried there. Perhaps it's because few folks will remember the lists. However, if leaders internalize via practice the ideas behind the numbers, then we can argue that leadership by the numbers is of more than passing value.

Let me close these reflections with my five "Cs" of conflict management:

- Confrontation: Look conflict in the eye and avoid third party conversations. Get the differences on the table.
- Communication: Make inquiries and insure that you have all facts and feelings relative to a conflict.
- Compassion: Don't make enemies of or demonize dissenters. You cannot hope that colleagues will give you the truth of your organization if they fear your reprisal or degradation.
- Cooperation: Separate people from issues where possible.
- Creation: Look for invention as a means of generating win-win or integrative solutions to conflicts before you escalate the conflict forum and lose decision discretion.

This closing note. There are some unhealthy personalities who are carriers of conflict, and there are some folks who may not have your health or the institution's health in mind. I have an administrative colleague and friend who kept a plaque on his office wall which read "Just because you are paranoid doesn't mean they are not out to get you!" For that occasional person who may be out to get you, I will have something to say about leadership responses in Chapter 8. Finally, there really are some intractable conflicts where we have to let the gentle waters of time rub off the hard edges of those conflicts, to live past and through those conflicts.

An organizational unit or campus without conflict is a dead organization, and a black crepe may be hung over both. An artistic college leader will welcome the opportunity to appreciate the outcomes of constructive conflict and to confront dysfunctional and destructive conflict.

## NOTES

1. Lee Bolman and Terrence Deal, *Reframing Organizations* (San Francisco, CA: Jossey Bass, 2003).

2. Gareth Morgan, *Images of Organization* (Thousand Oaks, CA: Sage Publications, 2006).

3. Mary Parker Follett, "Conflict," in *Mary Parker Follett: Prophet of Management*, ed. Pauline Graham (Boston, MA: Harvard Business School Press, 1996).

4. Kahlil Gibran, *Sand and Foam* (New York, NY: Alfred A. Knopf, 1973), 39.

5. Brian Muldoon, *The Heart of Conflict* (New York, NY: G.P. Putnam's Sons, 1996), 70.

6. Abraham Maslow, *The Farther Reaches of Human Nature* (New York, NY: The Viking Press, 1971).

# CHAPTER

# Radioactive Nurses and Reluctant Bursars: Evolutionary and Breakpoint Change in Higher Education

*The most embarrassing question that can be raised in a university is, what are we trying to do?*
—Robert Hutchins, *First Glimpses of a New World.*

*The task of the university is to weld together imagination and experience.*
—Alfred North Whitehead, *Universities and Their Functions*

In my sophomore year at what was then Memphis State College, I enrolled for the first general physics course under professor and department chair Dr. Carol Ijams. Outfitted in my air force blue ROTC uniform, I was sitting in the tiered seats attending Dr. Ijams' lecture on Newton's second law of motion and also working over a generous chew of Wrigley's spearmint gum.

Dr. Ijams was a colorful campus character, a captain in the naval reserve, perhaps 5′5″ in height, erect in military posture, and topped by a short cut of gray hair. He also had a high, piercing voice that could cut through ten feet of concrete. Turning from the blackboard and his extensive formulaic tour, he spotted me chewing the gum. He stopped his lecture, turned full front to the assembled class and said, "Damn, Grady! How do you expect to become an air force officer while chewing gum like an old cow?" He turned and continued his lecture while I sat seriously chagrined in my seat.

I yearned to slither away from his attention and that of my classmates, but seeing no way to escape with any sense of decorum, I simply removed the wad of gum and stuck it under the wooden chair seat. I never chewed gum in uniform ever thereafter.

Some dozen years later, I had completed a four-year tour with the air force, spent three years teaching physics for the U.S. Navy, completed my doctoral degree, returned to the University of Memphis first as Director of Records and Registration and then Director of Institutional Research. In addition to policy research, I held responsibility for design of institutional data systems. President C. C. "Sonny" Humphreys called me up to his office one day and gave me this problem to solve.

"Grady, we are running out of space in the social science building, and we need some place to move the nursing program. Check the space utilization in Manning Science Building and see if there's room for the nursing program in that building. If you are ready to do so, go over and talk to Dr. Ijams in the physics departments about the move."

Well, I had a space utilization report in my office revealing the use of every room on campus; and it didn't take long to discover that there were several classrooms available in Manning Hall, some not being used at all and others for only a class a day. There were also several vacant office spaces. The department of Biology had recently moved from Manning Hall to a newer building. And so away I went as facilities missionary to the office of Dr. Ijams, who was still chair of the physics department.

Perhaps anticipating that my visit was not about good news, he greeted me with cold demeanor and invited me to have a seat. Clutching my greenbar computer printout much like a security blanket, I opened the conversation as follows, "Dr. Ijams, President Humphreys is looking for a place to relocate the nursing program and he asked that I take a look at space utilization in Manning Hall. With a little planning, it seems that there might be several classrooms available, and there also appear to be several vacant offices."

Dr. Ijams launched from his desk chair and his emotion would have potentially carried him to the overhead ceiling tiles. Coming back to his chair, he turned to me and offered an invitation, or perhaps more a command, to leave his office, "You think you're gonna study a little physics with me, go off to the air force, come back here and with your computer reports, you're gonna tell me how to run this department and building. You just get your butt out of here!"

I left and went straight to the president's office. "Dr. Humphreys," I reported, "There's space in Manning Hall for the nursing program," and I showed him the utilization report. "Now Dr. Ijams was mad as hell when I went over to open an exploration of the possible move with him, so he's not gonna be initially very happy."

"But here's what you need to do and here's what will happen. You need to have the vice president for Academic Affairs, the dean of Arts and Science, and the Director of Facilities go ahead and plan the move. Initially, Dr. Ijams will prove resistant. But Dr. Ijams loves the ladies. Once the nursing faculty are in place, Dr. Ijams will be like a pig in a mud wallow, happy all the day long."

The next day, I made another tour through Manning Hall to check on some of the rooms on my utilization report and found on the door to each of the unused rooms a "Radiation Hazard" sign. When I peered into the room I could see a solitary instrument, such as a used Geiger counter or an abandoned Wilson Cloud chamber for tracking alpha particles or assorted other cast-off physics instruments. Dr. Ijams and others members of the physics faculty had taught me enough physics to recognize that this was a charade too hilarious to ignore, and so I went back to the President's office and gave him a report on what Dr. Ijams had done. I advised, however, that there was no danger of the nurses becoming radioactive and that the move should proceed.

Manning Hall was a classic, three-story brick building with a small external balcony located midway of the building on the second floor, and this balcony looked over a large parking lot for faculty and staff. About six months later, I came to work about 8:00 A.M. and parked in this lot. As I exited my car, I saw Dr. Ijams standing on the balcony, a little like the Pope of Manning Hall, greeting each and every female faculty member. In that high, piercing voice, he said, "Good morning, Sara! I don't know whether to stand up here and enjoy the view or come down there and enjoy your company!"

Whether in today's litigious climate this behavior might have approached a form of sexual harassment I'm not sure. Most of the nursing faculty had learned to joust with Dr. Ijams in the morning, to consider his morning greeting from the balcony harmless and a little spice for the day. And so Sara said, "Well, Carol, you just suit yourself," and went on her way to educate nurses.

## CHOREOGRAPHING THE DANCE OF CHANGE AND TRADITION

It's difficult for a college or university to bring about change in purpose, policy, or process. As with many other organizations, some of the change resistance reasons are personal and philosophical, some structural and political.

Prior to the previously outlined experience as Director of Institutional Research, I had an elementary test of leadership change and efficiency in my first appointment at Memphis State as a young registrar. I did not have to grapple with high level policy matters such as funding or affirmative action. What I did inherit was a registration system built to handle 2000 students with an enrollment trend in which the university was adding that many students every year during the baby boom years of the 1960s. Registration processes were snarled and students were mad.

As the new Lt. Fuzz of the University's registrar's office I was thrown head first into an angry mob of students, many of them walk-in traffic from the surrounding Memphis urban area, upset that they had no registration materials or that the materials they did have were not correct. After surviving one such trauma, I decided that once was enough. The president had indicated that I was to be in charge of registration, so I took charge. Like Brer Rabbit and the briar patch, I loved a good mess because I enjoyed organizing. And so we did.

Registration involved major coordination among academic departments, student services, and the finance/bursar's offices. We worked out an organization—and this was back in the punch-card, data input days—that would allow us to register about 800 students every twenty minutes. The first thing we had to throw overboard was the old alphabetical registration priority system, in which access to registration turned on the first letter in your last name. With many in the office decrying the loss of this tried and comfortable system, which was without any philosophical defense of equity or rationality, we lined up 20,000 students in the computer and arranged registration appointment times on the basis of cumulative hours earned. We gave first time freshman a break by registering them during the comfort and special guidance of summer orientation programs.

All was in readiness for the fall registration—save one office. The bursar, Mr. Lamar Newport, was not willing to leave the security of his two iron-caged windows in the administration building, and the newly designed registration system was about to dump over 2000 students every hour in front of those two windows.

I went to the president and explained to him the disaster that was about to occur and suggested that several hundred mad students would inevitably over-flow to his office just three or four doors down the hall in the administration building. The president intervened in kindly Godfather fashion and explained to Mr. Newport that he needed to join the system in the field house and prepare his clerks to receive the more than 2000 students that would come to him every hour. And so the Bursar left the comfort of his iron-window cages and came to the field house and set up his pay lines—several for cash, some for scholarships, some for credit cards.

We performed pilot runs of the system; and on the days of fall registration, all went without a hitch. I did, as a point of backup, station two of our most personable and persuasive student ambassadors in the president's office to han-dle any students who might run afoul of some process and decide that they would take their complaint to the president's office. These student goodwill and service ambassadors had to handle only a very small number of cases and did so with great effectiveness and caring.

This organizational and process innovation of the 1960s would look anti-quated today, due largely to information technology and organizational changes that have been adapted to serve students more effectively. With the application of computer and touch tone technology, registration processes today are cer-tainly more efficient and effective. Like our corporate colleagues, the new lead-ership challenge is to avoid customer technology rage in our touch-tone phone systems. These are designed to promote efficiency and good service but often produce just the opposite results, frustrating customers and clients along the way. Not all problems may match the touch-tone options provided, and not all touch-tone option systems provide a means of getting to a real live human being with a problem.

Other reasons for change resistance I outlined in my opening essay. An im-portant reason is that colleges and universities are not built to bob up and down on the waves and water of every passing fad that moves through society, whether that fad be one of educational or management practice. Colleges and universities are built for the long run. They are built, as I noted in my opening essay, to hold hands with the past and to reach for the future. Yet the lessons of history and contemporary life teach us that higher education has been responsive to change, sometimes responding to initiatives from without and sometimes from initiatives within.

The creation of the land grant university is attributed to the Land Grant Act of 1862, an external initiative, but the idea of the research university American scholars brought from Germany. "No better text for A History of Entrepreneurship could be found than the creation and development of the modern university, especially the modern American university" wrote Peter Drucker.[1] In Germany, according to Drucker, the concept of the university was an innovation whose impulse came from the influence of Prussian diplomat Wilhelm von Humboldt.[2] Americans married the research mission to the existing mission of teaching and learning we had transplanted from England and added the imminently practical mission of putting knowledge to work in the public service mission.

The emergence of the elective system within higher education in the later part of the 19th century and the development of extensive programs of continuing education in the latter part of the 20th century are primarily change initiatives that emerged from within. The evolution of normal schools and transformation of regional state colleges into state universities may be traced to partnership efforts between educators and political leaders and the policy pressure for access. At one time, the principal assumption of higher education was that learning took place only during the day. Private, mostly urban universities in northern cities were the first to venture into Evening Schools, offering courses at times and places more convenient to working students. It would be hard to find a public university or community college today that did not offer courses or programs in the evenings and on weekends.

Beyond the emergence of the research university, the evolution of state colleges, and the continuing vitality of the liberal arts/baccalaureate college, perhaps one of the most important American educational innovations is the two-year community and technical college. The birth of the two year college resides in the closing years of the 19th century but its most dramatic development clearly emerged in the latter third of the 20th century. The evolution of the modern university, the development of evening schools and programs, the creation of the contemporary two-year college, the design of extensive continuing education programs, the experiment with network, on-line programs—these are ventures and institutional responses to new markets, new students, and new technology. The development of the proprietary college is a story still unfolding in American higher education. Clearly, American higher education is not a static work in its programs, its policies, or its processes.

The pressure and call for change remain unabated, however, and there is no reason to excuse universities from the pressure to change. The June 2, 2006 issue of The Chronicle of Higher Education carried a major story entitled "A Texas Millionaire Plots the Future of Higher Education," and the front page of this issue carried a picture of Charles Miller as "The Tough Texan Who Wants to Change Academe."[3] Mr. Miller chaired the Secretary of Education's Commission on the Future of Higher Education. In the article, author Kelly Field described Mr. Miller's posture on higher education as follows:

> From that post (as Chairman of the federal commission), he has poked, prodded, and sometimes provoked academe, challenging its "complacent," change resistant culture and calling for it to become more accountable to families and taxpayers. He scoffs at the notion that "only the high priesthood of academia" knows how to improve higher education, arguing that colleges could learn a lot from the business world.[4]

Are those of us who serve in collegiate leadership positions "change resistant" and so arrogant and narrow minded that we think we are the only ones that know how to improve colleges and universities? That's not been my experience. It has been my experience that friends in corporate leadership are occasionally afflicted with the idea that only the incentive of profit can induce the search for improved effectiveness and efficiency. The spirit and incentive of service and duty, the knowledge that you are steward of civic generosity and trustee of taxpayer support, and the pride of craftsmanship are powerful motivators for public sector leaders.

There are several possible reactions to Mr. Miller's reflections. One is that recommended by Ralph Waldo Emerson, who noted that it is in our best interest to throw ourselves on the side of our assailants to see what we might learn from them. The second is that indeed sometimes change will be imposed from outside, and the applause will perhaps come later after the merit of the change is proved.

A third reaction is that folks who live in glass houses should not be throwing bricks at others. Robert Birnbaum has written an engaging and informing book on *Management Fads in Higher Education* in which he commented that:

> When critics of higher education ask, "Why can't a college be more like a business?" they are likely to take a narrow perspective. They refer to business's presumed efficiency, but they usually ignore business's penchant for short-term expediency and golden parachutes. They overlook the selection of board members by management, provision of stock options to failed executives, and CEO salaries unrelated to company performance and over four hundred times the average factory worker.[5]

Which business management practices would Mr. Miller like for higher education leaders to emulate? Those of executives from Enron, Tyco, Health South? Or perhaps those of Chrysler Motors in the early 1980s when the Federal Government held the company alive with loan guarantees? Or perhaps those practices of the executives of the nation's savings and loan industry, who in the 1980s and 1990s cost the taxpayers of this nation over $124 billion to clean up the debris from the collapsed financial institutions. Or perhaps those of companies and their executives who conspire to fix prices or overcharge government for goods and services? Or those of the tobacco industry who kept silent on the cancerous effects of smoking?

It might be possible to get folks to change by hitting them in the face with a wet squirrel. On the other hand, you may also make them mad as hell. In the opening year of the 21st century, I wrote:

> Would we in higher education take as mission the education of men and women who have both the will and the competence for critical thought, who live with that energizing little word "why" hiding in mind and heart and simultaneously expect the abode of their intellectual incubation to be exempt from the scrutiny of those whom we have taught to be curious?[6]

There is a connection between corporate and collegiate organizations that may be overlooked by those of us in collegiate leadership. Why should collegiate leaders be offended at criticism flowing from civic and corporate leaders when, as I earlier noted, we have trained our graduates to such critical dispositions? And why should we be offended, when we are leaders of an enterprise built to bring policy and practice in every field of endeavor under critical scrutiny and evaluation? How are we able to do that? We are able to do that because the profits of a market economy provide tax support and private donor generosity to our colleges and universities. As London Financial Times economics writer Martin Wolf notes, "The market economy does not merely support its critics, it embraces them."[7] It is no small wonder that our democratic and market economy society is willing to support an enterprise to be critical of itself.

For those who furnish leadership in higher education, a healthy response to criticism and change pressure does not require collegiate leaders to bend over and invite colleagues in the corporate sector to kick us for what they perceive as complacent and inefficient practices. It might be argued that there is plenty of inside work to be done in both collegiate and corporate sectors before we invest our energy in cleaning up the other fellow's back yard. A more constructive leadership response for collegiate leaders is to attend carefully the criticism lofted at the academy, to invite partnerships of thought and action in which the traffic of good ideas may flow in a two-way thoroughfare between our colleges and our corporations, and to actively embrace the breakpoint moment that may be upon us.

As earlier noted, collegiate leaders hold in trust an enterprise of complex and tensioned mission, of complicated governance processes, of outcomes and goals that cannot be carried in a single number or metric, of complicated quality/ accountability definitions and evidence, of cultures of faith and fact. Not the least of the challenges college leaders face is choreographing the dance of tradition and change, of honoring heritage while both leading and responding to change. Nor is this challenge of leadership balance going to become any easier as we move into the 21st century. Before I move to consideration of that possible breakpoint moment in the life of higher education, I would like to attend briefly one other important point related to conflict and change.

## DEMONIZING THE DISSENTER

In my career as both administrator and professor, I have seen the movement from large scale computers occupying entire rooms to the same computing capacity carried in the palm of your hand. I have seen an extraordinary expansion of higher education institutional size, types and programs. I have seen the emergence of policies designed to eliminate discrimination on economic, racial, gender, and disability bases. I have seen major changes in governance arrangements, especially for public institutions.

In that career I have experienced both the challenge and the pleasure associated with major program and policy changes in the positions and organizations I served. As earlier noted, in my first position at the University of Memphis, we re-organized registration and information data systems. We participated in development of the state's first financial formula allocation policy to promote equitable distribution of public funds, a policy offering a more rational and equitable allocation than past dependence on presidential lobbying power. At the Tennessee Higher Education Commission, I directed the Performance Funding project which gave birth to the first state policy allocating some state funds on a performance rather than an enrollment policy. This policy, now in its twenty-fifth year, is a policy venture I explore more fully in Chapter 12. When I became chancellor at LSU Shreveport, the University was one of a half dozen schools in the South that pilot tested new institutional effectiveness accreditation criteria and processes.

On that note related to accreditation, here's a bulletin. Some of those associated with the USOE 2006 report "A Test of Leadership: Charting the Future of Higher Education" (The Spellings Report)[8] and some of those commenting on the report have criticized regional accreditation for being process oriented—counting library books, square footage, and number of Ph.Ds. While well intended, some of these critics must have been living in locations where sunlight has to be sent in by pipleine, or in some intellectual isolation. I've been chairing accrediting visits for the Commission on Colleges for the Southern Association of Colleges and Schools since the early 1980s, and we haven't worked on such narrow criteria for more than twenty years.

Many books have been written on the theme of change. Alvin Tolfler's 1871 *Future Shock*[9] was an early version, followed by Rosbeth Moss Kanter's 1984 *The Change Masters*,[10] George Land and Beth Jarman's 1992 *Breakpoint and Beyond*,[11] James O'Toole's 1995 *Leading Change*,[12] and William Bridges' 2003 *Managing Transitions*.[13] These are by no means the universe of commentary on this topic.

The following reflection will be a grossly oversimplified summary of those works and change research, but basically the two important ideas seem to be these. If you want successful, long-term change, you must involve those whose welfare will be affected, whose intelligence and energy will enrich the change process, and whose talent and allegiance will be central to the sustenance of the change. In contrast, there are moments when limits of time and resources and when moral imperative calls for top down and command-force change to avoid fiscal/performance disaster and to eliminate human and organizational degradation caused by leaders taking their personnel and organizations in harm's way because of personal duplicity.

Beyond the cultural complexities of mission tension and governance processes, colleges and universities face the same resistance points to change as other organizations. There is personal resistance framed in concern for security, organizational resistance framed into the veto effect of bureaucratic organizations, conceptual resistance framed in fear of the unknown, political resistance framed in loss or gain of influence and power, and philosophical resistance framed in honest dissent over purpose and process.

On this last point of resistance, I note again that one of the less savory and less effective leadership responses to those who disagree with us is to demonize the opposition. There is a triple sadness for collegiate leaders afflicted with this view. First is the sadness associated with the inability to deal with honest dissent in an organization whose culture and mission essence are built on honest dissent. Second, is the sadness that comes from seeing leaders deprive themselves of access to the truth about their organizations because they repress disagreement. Third is the sadness that flows from the loss of intelligence and creativity when colleagues shackle their minds and hearts because dissent is not tolerated.

## A BREAKPOINT MOMENT FOR HIGHER EDUCATION

I like the three-stage model of organization change proposed by Land and Jarman, whose 1992 book I earlier cited. There is first the "Organizational Forming" stage marked by creative and entrepreneurial spirit. This is followed by the "Organizational Norming" stage marked by codification, policy formulation, and standardization. The third is "Organizational Reforming" marked by either organizational demise or reinvention and innovation. Movement among these three stages is seen as a "breakpoint" moment.

Those living in any time or age can never be sure that leadership challenges are easier or more complicated than the past. The oxymoron expression "chronic crisis" does seem to fit higher education. Has there ever been a moment in the life of American higher education when some fault of policy or practice was not perceived by one or more stakeholders, whether internal or external? Are the challenges facing American higher education today more dramatic than those faced during and following the Civil War, during the Great Depression, or immediately after World War II?

I don't know the answer. It does seem to me, however, that collegiate leaders in the near future may be facing a potential breakpoint moment in the life of higher education. This breakpoint moment is associated first with the systems surrounding higher education. There are social changes of growing ethnic diversity and family structure. There are rapid technological changes. There are political changes around the world. There are economic changes associated with globalization and international interdependence. There are potential environmental changes with global warming. There are revolution imprints associated with a growing distance between the wealthy and those on factory shop floors. There are unimaginable and frequent events of genocide reaching over the 20th century that one would not associate with what should be a more civilized world. There is unpredictable violence in the presence of world wide terrorism.

As Land and Jarman noted in their book, "The kind of transformation that leads to the reinvention of any ongoing enterprise is usually totally neglected. This is why the airplane industry was not invented by the railroads."[14] Higher education is also not immune from a revolutionary educational idea.

Ideas matter. Ideas are important. And higher education is in the business of ideas. Our ideological paradigms—our philosophical assumptions, frames of reference, and ways of thinking—shape our realities. One might argue that higher education has experienced paradigm shifts in mission and types of institutions, in attitudes on student access, in notions of quality and accountability, in finance and revenue policy, and in governance arrangements.

Important philosophical foundations of higher education are under active scrutiny:

- Should the concept of faculty tenure be abandoned?
- Should we charge differential tuition among fields of study?
- Should we manage the university more like a corporation . . . or vice versa?
- Should all colleges and universities become proprietary institutions and the idea of the state supported or state assisted college/university be jettisoned?
- Should public accountability expectations be moderated or dissolved if the state reduces its financial support?
- Should public governance structures be amended so that there is sufficient authority strength for boards to harness institutional status goals to state goals and resources?
- Should we continue to honor and insist upon varieties of excellence among institutions of differential mission or shall we cast quality into the single data point of reputation?
- Should we "unbundle" payment for educational services?
- Should the state pay only for instruction and federal government/corporations for research?
- Should public service become totally client supported or remain a state/federal obligation?
- Should students pay only for those student services they desire?
- Should intercollegiate athletics become a tub on its own revenue bottom, with either donors or students paying by choice and not by mandate?

There are also policy issues related to such themes as affirmative action and financial aid that, when added to the aforementioned questions, may mark this as a breakpoint moment for higher education. College and universities are not only in the business of ideas, they are in the business of equipping men and women with the will and capacity to frame good questions, and we ourselves should embrace the challenge of change carried in these questions. Trustees of colleges and universities should be open to criticism but not without conviction on the heritage and promise of the organization they hold in trust. Conviction furnishes the leadership and ideological platform from which we may discern both error and new truth.

## NOTES

1. Peter Drucker, *Innovation and Entrepreneurship* (New York, NY: Harper and Row, 1985), 23.

2. Ibid., 177.

3. Kelly Field, "A Texas millionaire plots the future of higher education," *The Chronicle of Higher Education*. LI , no. 39 (June 2, 2006): A16–A18.

4. Ibid., A16.

5. Robert Birnbaum, *Management Fads in Higher Education* (San Francisco, CA: Jossey-Bass Publishers, 2000), xiii.

6. E. Grady Bogue, E. and Jeffrey Aper, *Exploring the Heritage of American Higher Education* (San Francisco, CA: Jossey-Bass Publishers, 2000), 204.

7. Martin Wolf, *Why Globalization Works* (New Haven, CT: Yale University Press, 2005), 55.

8. *A Test of Leadership: Charting the Future of U.S. Higher Education. A Report of the Commission Appointed by Secretary of Education Margaret Spellings*, (Washington, D.C.: United States Office of Education, September 2006).

9. Alvin Tofler, *Future Shock* (New York, NY: Bantam, 1976).

10. Rosabeth Moss Kanter, *The Change Masters* (New York, NY: Touchstone-Simon and Schuster, 1983).

11. George Land and Beth Jarman, *Breakpoint and Beyond* (New York, NY: Harper Business, 1992).

12. James O'Toole, *Leading Change* (San Francisco, CA: Jossey-Bass Publishers, 1995).

13. William Bridges, *Managing Transitions* (Cambridge, MA: DeCapo Press, 2003).

14. Land and Jarman, *Breakpoint and Beyond*, 29.

# CHAPTER

# New Chancellor on Campus:
# The Leader as
# Constructive Pessimist

*Life has taught me—and this is my luck—that active loving saves me from a morbid preoccupation with the shortcomings of society and the waywardness of men.*

—Alan Paton, *The Challenge of Fear*

*Our Founders were constructive pessimists to the degree that they constantly thought about what might go wrong in human relations.*

—Robert Kaplan, *Warrior Politics*

In the 1980s, following an extended executive search process, I was appointed chancellor of Louisiana State University in Shreveport (LSUS). When the appointment was announced in Nashville, Tennessee, where I was then serving as Associate Executive Director of the Tennessee Higher Education Commission, news accounts revealed that several administrators on the LSU-Shreveport campus had been candidates for the position.

Having that knowledge, a presidential friend called me in Nashville and asked, "Grady, who are you taking with you to Shreveport?" "Well," I replied, "there will be my wife Linda and our collie dog, Moses." Thinking of the seven folks on campus who had been candidates, he advised that I was going to need a friend in Shreveport. I thought not. I would go to Shreveport expecting the best from every man and woman there. I would not demean the performance investment of men and women there by going in with saber drawn nor would I burden their promise with my prejudice. If there was a betrayal of that expectation and trust, I would deal with it at the moment.

There are, of course, new college presidents who bring other attitudes to their positions and who design other leadership realities. Some presidents will enter an institution and immediately request letters of resignation from all administrators reporting to them. Apparently the theory is that the new leader has the right to form his or her own team and needs the opportunity to discern who will stay and who will go. Having a letter of resignation in hand foregoes any need for compassion and courage and any real need for performance discernment. This approach, however, may reflect more the fear and the insecurity of a new president than any healthy philosophy of leadership.

Is there any principle of human behavior more powerful in its application than the power of our expectations? Leadership texts celebrate the power of expectancy theory, advising that positive images create positive realities. Holding in one hand the attracting power of high expectations, leaders call on noble motives and act to design constructive realities. Alert to the reality of dark and selfish motives, however, the artistic and effective leader holds in the other hand the discovery promise of financial and performance audits, the cultivation of informal intelligence networks, and the corrective promise of courage in confronting duplicity, arrogance, and prejudice.

As noted in Chapter 2, writing in his 2002 book *Warrior Politics: Leadership and a Pagan Ethos*, Robert D. Kaplan[1] described the political architects of America as "constructive pessimists." They designed a government built on the civic wisdom of the people. The framework they put in place, however, was also designed to guard against abuses of power, to recognize the negative valence of self interests, and to answer the pleas of those seeking redress for injustice. There was no hiding from the shadow side of human nature in the Constitution.

In any organizational enterprise, how does the effective leader realize the constructive advantage of optimistic expectations, affirming noble behavioral motives but anticipating the possibility of mean and shadow motives at work? Let's examine the possibilities of the "constructive pessimist" metaphor for leader role.

## OPTIMISM: THE BEST AND MOST PHILOSOPHIC INVENTION OF MIND

Over twenty years ago I spoke to the power of leadership expectations in these reflections:

> We can enshrine mediocrity or promote excellence, tie down every Gulliver or free human potential. What differences in the behavior of our students would we predict if we expect success rather than failure? What difference in faculty performance do we elicit if we expect responsibility rather than apathy? And what record do we establish if we expect trust rather than deviousness? We may have the dubious pleasure of always being surprised if we consistently underestimate the potential of those with whom we work, but we can never know what the far limit of that potential might have been.[2]

In 1943, Harry Hopkins, one of President Roosevelt's closest confidants, was helping the president prepare his State of the Union message. War production targets were a central piece of the speech, and Hopkins had used the best estimate of experts in projecting that the United States would build 24,000 planes that year. Roosevelt told Hopkins to double that number and add 12,000. The United States did not build 60,000 planes in 1944, but American workers did built 49,000, a figure twice the expert prediction.

The power of optimism and high expectations is nicely anchored in philosophy, science, and art. The German philosopher and poet Johann Goethe observed that "When we take people merely as they are, we make them worse; when we treat them as if they were what they should be, we improve them as far as they can be improved."[3]

The original scientific evidence for expectancy theory in human relations has what some might consider an unflattering heritage. The principle emerged from the work of psychologist Robert Rosenthal and associates in training rats to run a maze.[4] After giving two groups of graduate students rats to work with, telling one group that their rats were "bright" and suggesting to a second group that their rates were "not bright," the psychologists found that the maze-running time of those rats described as bright was significantly shorter than the second group. When observing and questioning the graduate students, they found that students with the so called "bright rats" were more affirming and enthusiastic as they described their attitudes in working with the rats.

Rosenthal took these results and replicated the experiment in a small elementary school. One group of teachers was told that they would be working with students ready to blossom and full of promise, but said nothing about the promise of students to a second group of teachers. As with the rats, there was no significant difference in the ability of the children at the beginning of the experiment. At the end of the school year, however, the students described as "intellectually blooming" scored significant gains in IQ measurements. Studies of expectations have been replicated in a variety of management and employee environments, such as banking and insurance, with similar improvement in performance results.

Rosenthal's work was reported in a 1968 book authored with Lenore Jacobson entitled *Pygmalion in the Classroom*.[5] The word *Pygmalion* leads nicely to the artistic support for high expectations as carried in George Bernard Shaw's play *Pygmalion* and its musical adaptation in Lerner and Loewe's *My Fair Lady*. The transformation of Eliza Doolittle from a rough-edged, cockney flower girl into a classical lady of English society is the story of both the play and the musical. The revealing quotation by Eliza Doolittle late in the play cuts to the heart of the human relations principle: "You see, really and truly, apart from the things anyone can pick up (the dressing and the proper way of speaking, and so on), the difference between a lady and a flower girl is not how she behaves, but how she's treated."[6]

If the evidence for the power of optimism and high expectations gleaned from the pages of philosophy, science, and art were not enough, readers with religious inclination might find the Old Testament book Numbers, Chapter 13, of interest. The twelve Israelites sent on reconnaissance to the land of Canaan saw the same people and conditions in Canaan. However, two different views were imposed on those observations, a defeated view and a "we are well able to overcome" view.

Effective leaders bring an expectant touch of optimism to their work and design climates in which excellence and integrity are expected from each and every one in the organization. High expectations apply first to leaders themselves. As we will explore more fully in Chapter 8, the sad behaviors reported in the *Wall Street Journal* and other media outlets in recent years on corporate executives at Enron, World Comm, American Airlines, Tyco, in non-profit agencies such as United Way, and in some universities portray a condition of soul erosion in too many management suites. Leaders are unlikely to realize the power of high expectations without exemplifying the same expectations in their own lives.

There are important caveats to consider as one nurtures the power latent in high expectations. First, expecting others to do their best is not the same as ensuring success, is not the same as making achievement look easy, and should not be used to make others the prisoners of our expectations. Designing climates of civility and responsibility is the work of the leadership optimist. But what of possible betrayal by the few with more self-serving and destructive motives? How will leaders prepare for the occasional reality of negative and shadow motives among those for whom they are responsible?

## CONSTRUCTIVE PESSIMISM: ALERTNESS AND COURAGE

A first act is to avoid living in a pollyanna cocoon and to understand that some folks may choose to live by selfish and destructive motives. One might think that the clash of motives, the combat of nobility and evil as depicted in great literature and music, in religious thought, and in experience would be sufficient to guard against such naiveté. Not so.

After several years of effective service in a large, nonprofit organization, an executive friend of mine was relieved from duty by his board because he failed to discipline one of his vice presidents, who was feeding members of the board false and negative feedback on the executive and who hoped that he might then be appointed to the position. My executive friend found it difficult to accept the reality of this betrayal and took no action to confront and correct the offending vice president.

Second, the leader needs the courage to confront betrayal and duplicity. In his essay on *Courage*, Ralph Waldo Emerson (1929) wrote that "There is a courage of the cabinet as well as a courage of the field; a courage of manners in private assemblies and another in public assemblies; a courage which enables one man to speak masterly to a hostile company, whilst another man who can easily face a cannon's mouth dares not open his own."[7]

Whether on the battlefield or in the boardroom, whether confronting a major organizational challenge or a wayward colleague, courage links knowledge of what is right to decision and action based on that knowledge. This is the heart of Stephen Carter's definition of integrity in his 1997 book entitled *Integ-*

*rity.*[8] It may be that exemplary leaders do not think so much about being coura-geous as they do about honoring moral principle. Thus, the absence of courage may be a condition of moral bankruptcy, an absence of caring for excellence and integrity. In the earlier cases of wayward corporate executives, financial bankruptcy was a predictable outcome of moral bankruptcy. The leader as con-structive pessimist does not shrink from corrective action in the face of wrong-doing.

The president of a large public university relieved the dean of his medical school from duty upon learning that the medical school and its associate hospi-tal had admitted patients for organ transplants with the full knowledge that these patients would probably not get transplants. The president successfully fought opposition from the governor of the state and many in the state's medi-cal profession and was supported by his governing board in dealing with this sad case of professional duplicity. Here were medical professionals whose oath was to do no harm but whose behavior betrayed the oath.

Third, the leader will arrange for independent acquisition of intelligence on the performance of the organization and its personnel. Financial and perfor-mance audits are perhaps the most obvious and most formal expressions of such intelligence. There are sad cases in which accounting firms expected to render independent corporate audits were found to be in collusion. There must be unquestioned independence in this relationship. Who will guard the guardians is not an empty query.

There is one other political and preventive step leaders can take to anticipate unresponsive behavior to high expectations. Recognizing the political reality of organizations requires that the leader be a student of influence and that he or she exhibit the capacity to be personal. In a world of memos and email it is easy to be impersonal, and it is easier to be suspicious of those we know only at a distance. Interpersonal relationships that carry bonds of trust can also serve as useful informal information networks.

Borrowing a line from another musical "The King and I," when I moved to take appointment as Chancellor of LSU in Shreveport I first invested internal "getting- to-know you" time with vice chancellors, deans, department chairs, and with faculty and student leadership. I then moved into the Shreveport metropolitan community by scheduling lunches and breakfasts for one-on-one conversations with civic and business leaders.

When I had lunch with the mayor or the president of the chamber of com-merce, I would ask them to suggest a couple of other influential voices in the city that I should get to know. Over the year, I had personal fellowship with a large number of folks, some of whom occupied highly visible and formal leader-ship positions and others who did not hold formal position but whose influence was such that when they opened their mouths, many in the city listened.

This investment of time and caring allowed me to establish personal rela-tionships with many folks throughout the community's economic, social, and cultural structure. Second, it built a network of personal and information con-nections so that I had ready intelligence on any person or policy moving in the community that might involve the university. It also became a way for me to become involved in various civic organizations and invested in the welfare of the city. Another positive outcome of this "getting to know you" tactic I will report in Chapter 9.

I experienced a second opportunity to deploy the philosophy of leadership carried in these reflections as I was called in 1989 by the LSU Board of Supervisors and LSU system President Alan Copping to be the interim chancellor at the research university campus of the LSU system. During my first days on campus I was given cultural orientation and told that the official name of the campus was Louisiana State University and Agricultural and Mechanical College.

The campus had become badly split over the sudden resignation of its chancellor, who had created a confrontation with the University's graduate faculty over the dismissal and readmission of a doctoral student. Apparently the graduate faculty had dismissed the student for academic reasons; and the readmission by the chancellor had political overtones, as the student was the daughter of a prominent political leader. Leadership attitudes among the college deans were split, and the provost and the Faculty Senate president would hardly speak to one another. This conflict of opinion over the departure conditions of the chancellor had spilled over into a conflict over who would serve as interim chancellor, some wanting the campus provost and some wanting the system vice president for Academic Affairs to be named interim chancellor.

Understandably anxious about further polarization of the campus, the Board and president asked if I would be willing to come down from Shreveport and serve as interim chancellor. I agreed to do so, but not without some decision agony in our family. My wife Linda remained in Shreveport with our three small children—ages 8, 6, and 4. She was the heroine of this decision, as I departed Shreveport on Monday mornings at 4:00 AM for the 200-mile drive to Baton Rouge and returned on Friday evenings at 9:00 PM. The eight month separation was moderated by occasional visits of Linda and children to Baton Rouge.

I remember sitting in my car just outside the ornate entry gate to the LSU Baton Rouge campus on January 2, 1989, wondering what challenges I would face on this complex research university campus of 26,000 students. I shoved a tape of the sound track from "Superman" into the cassette deck and drove onto the campus like I knew what I was doing.

Again, I entered the assignment determined to expect the very best of every man and woman there, regardless of their position on the performance of the previous chancellor. Equally willing was I, however, to confront the wayward behavior of any colleague who betrayed his or her integrity and my trust. Difficult issues of budget and revenue, intercollegiate athletics, university admission policy were constructively engaged, and folks with strained relationships learned to work together on these.

There were two events, however, that called for blunt force action. One was the firing of the University's director of finance who had conspired with a clerk in the financial aid office to embezzle $50,000 from the University. Obviously, high expectations and trust had failed with this director. The presence of an effective internal audit and an alert vice chancellor for Financial Affairs had ferreted out the wrongdoing. How pleased I was to have a "constructive pessimist" as vice chancellor for Financial Affairs, an administrative colleague who held high expectations of his staff but who kept his audits active.

A second unhappy example turned on the behavior of the director of a major research facility, the Center for Advanced Micro Electronic Devices (CAMD). The University had received a $25 million federal grant to build a synchrotron facility, a 25-meter racetrack for electrons in which bending magnets accelerated electrons around the track, with electrons giving off X-rays as they were accelerated. The relatively young, mid thirties research scientist directing the design of this project was ignoring the advice of a stellar advisory panel composed of the Science and the Engineering deans and several senior level professors. More importantly, he had a serious alcohol problem and when drunk would threaten to beat up any person within reach. This became more than a little serious when at a National Science Foundation conference he apparently threatened the head of the NSF.

Technical, social, and political complications included these factors. First there was apprehension that the director was one of few people in the country who had a good knowledge of synchrotron accelerator facilities. My feeling, however, was that we could not be intimidated by his lock on knowledge. There had to be more than one person who understood synchrotrons.

A second implication was that the young scientist was friends with several of Senator Bennett Johnston's personal staff, the senator having been instrumental in helping attract the federal grant; and he was a personal friend of a West German scientist in Hamburg, whom the university was trying to recruit to operate the facility.

Having tried to persuade the director to get help for his alcoholism and failing, I collected a very bright and articulate associate dean of engineering and two senior faculty in physics and caught a plane to Washington, DC, where I explained to Senator Johnston that I was going to fire the young scientist, told him why, and pledged that the facility would be built on time and his role in helping attract the center would be honored. The senator said he understood, that he had just voted against Texas Senator John Tower for Secretary of Defense for the same reason (alcoholism), and that I should return to LSU and do what was right.

I returned to Baton Rouge and with the associate dean as companion caught a plane to Hamburg, Germany. There at dinner on the Elbe River, we explained the problem to our German physicist and asked whether he was still willing to come to Baton Rouge to run the facility if his friend were no longer there. He was. I shoved a contract across the table, signed him up, came home, and relieved the director from duty.

As a postscript, the young associate dean I pulled into action, Dr. Harvill Eaton, later served for several years as provost/vice president of Drexel University and is now serving as president of Cumberland University in Lebanon, Tennessee.

## "IF MEN WERE ANGELS . . ."

"If men were angels, no government would be necessary," wrote James Madison in *Federalist No. 51*. If all organizational colleagues were of noble intent, leaders could travel primarily on high expectations and not think about the "constructive pessimist" metaphor of leadership role.

Former President Andrew "Andy" Holt of the University of Tennessee frequently complimented his staff in public remarks. If you were one of those who had done your work well, you could take pleasure in this recognition. If you were one of those who had not, and you listened carefully, you could quickly discover what it was the president wished you to be doing better. Beyond his considerable and widely known public speaking skill, combining humor and substance, Andy Holt was a collegiate leader of great charm and competence who brought a simple but powerful impulse to his role—hire smart people and let them do their work.

Holding high expectations is a deliberate leadership design that accords nicely with a view of leadership role that accents the earlier described "inquire and inspire" leadership role over a "tell and compel" role view. The leader asks more questions and gives fewer orders, invites colleagues to responsibility in framing purpose and evaluating performance, and invests them with his or her trust. The "constructive pessimist" leader, however, is alert to potentially selfish motives and wayward behavior and is perfectly willing to adopt a "tell and compel" style when that is needed to correct behavior and/or to arrange consequences for those who steal property or promise from their organizations or colleagues.

## NOTES

1. Robert Kaplan, *Warrior Politics: Why Leadership Demands a Pagan Ethos* (New York, NY: Random House, 2002).

2. E. Grady Bogue, *The Enemies of Leadership* (Bloomington, IN: Phi Delta Kappa, 1985), 18–19.

3. Johann Goethe, *Wilhelm Meister's Apprenticeship* (New York, NY: The Heritage Press, 1959), 497.

4. Robert Rosenthal, "The Pygmalion Effect Lives," *Psychology Today* (September, 1973), 56–63.

5. Robert Rosenthal and Lenore Jacobson, *Pygmalion in the Classroom* (New York, NY: Holt, Rinehart and Winston, 1968).

6. George Bernard Shaw, *Pygmalion* (New York, NY: Signet Classics, 1975).

7. Ralph Waldo Emerson, "Courage," *The complete writings of Ralph Waldo Emerson. Volume 1* (New York, NY: Morrow, 1929).

8. Stephen Carter, *Integrity* (New York, NY: HarperCollins Publishers, 1996).

# CHAPTER

## Soul Erosion and Executive Empathy: The Seduction of Leadership Conscience

*To feel with another is to care. In this sense, the opposite of empathy is antipathy. The empathetic attitude is engaged again and again in moral judgments, for moral dilemmas involve potential victims.*
                                          —Daniel Goleman, *Emotional Intelligence*

*. . . why must a society accept a capitalism that persists in generating greater inequities, generation after generation, as the required terms for sustaining general abundance?*
                                          —William Greider, *The Soul of Capitalism*

When the performance and effectiveness of college leaders are assessed, will that assessment address only unit/organizational goal achievement and perhaps the satisfaction and confidence of the stakeholders to whom the leader is responsible? John Gardner suggests that "Ultimately, we judge our leaders in a framework of values."[1] Many leaders are arguably both efficient and effective in achieving unworthy and/or immoral goals, and Gardner profiles a sad litany from Klu Klux Klan leaders in America to Idi Amin in Africa. Surely, history offers a seriously contrasting leadership effectiveness story for Winston Churchill than for Adolf Hitler, a different narrative for Franklin Roosevelt than for Josef Stalin.

Indeed, if one accepts our proposition of Chapter 2, that leadership is a moral art form, then the moral and ethical influence of leaders is a front-and-center matter, and more so for those leading our colleges and universities, institutions expected to prepare leadership for every sector of our national life. That those who follow yearn for integrity in their leaders is made clear in the research presented by James Kouzes and Barry Posner in their book *Credibility* in which we find such value adjectives as honest, fair-minded, courageous, and caring to describe the credible leader.[2]

In graduate programs designed for the education of those who will carry leadership responsibility in American colleges and universities, the faculty at the University of Tennessee hold before our students this preface and core values that undergird study at the University of Tennessee:

> The effectiveness of leaders at any level and in any setting turns on competency and conscience. Technical knowledge and skill are placed in action in the service of values, which are premier design instruments for organizational cultures and climates. Honoring these core values promotes leadership effectiveness. Neglecting these values places client and organizations in harm's way and diminishes the meaning and performance of the university—its faculty, staff, and students.

- Civility—Affirming the power of human dignity and diversity
- Candor—Respecting the power of public forum and the role of dissent and debate
- Responsibility—Accepting care for one's actions and decisions
- Compassion—Caring for person and principle and holding high expectations
- Community—Respecting diversity while developing an agenda of common caring
- Persistence—Accenting long range goals and staying the course in the face of hardship
- Service—Placing the welfare and promise of others before self
- Excellence—Calling individuals and organizations to high standards of Performance
- Justice—Insuring equity and opportunity and recognition

Students have the right to hold our faculty accountable to these same values! That we have an important and continuing work on this theme will be apparent as one examines the recent record of both corporate and collegiate leaders. Let us turn there.

## SOUL EROSION IN EXECUTIVE SUITES

The September 19, 2003, issue of *The Chronicle of Higher Education* carried a front page story on tuition policy options currently being explored in higher education, as higher education responds to serious revenue squeezes in both public and private sectors.

Commenting on and criticizing our proclivity to look at tuition increases as the first response to resource pressures, Mark Yudof, Chancellor of the University of Texas System, remarked in this same September 19, 2003, issue of the *Chronicle* that "If American Airlines hired an outside consultant to tell them how to increase profits, and the suggestion was only to raise prices, the consultant would probably be fired."[3]

The use and timing of this illustration involving American Airlines is curious and perhaps regrettable. American Airlines had been featured in an earlier 2003 issue of *The Wall Street Journal* for the behavior of its board and executives, who were busy arranging multi-million dollar retention bonuses and pension benefits for corporate executives while the company was asking employees of the airline to take pay cuts of 15 percent to 23 percent to forestall the airline filing for bankruptcy.[4]

What vision, what metaphor of leadership role and responsibility could have been guiding these trustees and executives of American Airlines? What values anchored their action? Surely it was not the "servant-leader" metaphor popularized by Robert Greenleaf and so frequently advanced in current leadership literature.[5] Surely they would not be considered moral exemplars. This leadership behavior represents a sad case of soul erosion in corporate executive suites. For these executives, the "arrogance" meter would have pegged to the red zone, and the "empathy" meter would have read zero, should such value metrics have been available. These are executives that John Gardner, author of *Excellence*, would describe as "champions of exploitation" and "virtuosos of avarice."[6]

Such leadership behavior deserves a "Rotten Oscar" award for executive hubris and insensitivity, though there would be other lively corporate contenders from World Comm, Enron, Health South, Tyco, and Adelphia. Earlier works *In the Name of Profit* by Robert Heilbroner,[7] *Den of Thieves* by James Stewart,[8] and contemporary works such as *Pigs at the Trough* by Arianna Huffington,[9] have detailed what happens when the pursuit of profit and the force of greed shove aside integrity and empathy. Readers will find the more recent story of Enron as carried in *Conspiracy of Fools* by Kenneth Eichenwald[10] equally interesting. Parenthetically, in 1980 the typical corporate president was paid 42 times as much as the average worker in America. In 2001, it was 530 times as much![11]

As further commentary on corporate executive pay, an editorial in the January 8, 2007, issue of *USA Today* suggested that Americans might understand multi million dollar nest eggs given to retiring executives when a company has been doing well, though the size of such nest eggs, running in the $150 to $400 million range, would defy imagination for most Americans. When CEO's, however, are given $200 million golden parachutes when their companies have been in the economic doldrums, the editorial by Alejandro Gonzalez comments that such rewards "dispel the argument that executive pay is rational or fair."[12] A subsequent letter to the editor about this editorial described it as misguided and anti-American.

The January 27, 2006, issue of *The Knoxville News Sentinel* reported that a disturbing income gap was continuing to develop in Tennessee. The paper reported that in the period from 1980 to 2003, the increase in average income for the bottom fifth of Tennesseans was 18.6 percent, whereas the increase in income for the top fifth of Tennesseans was 70.9 percent.[13] This widening divide in compensation between executives and those on the firing line, corporate or collegiate, is an incendiary trend and appears to be a trend which some higher education boards of trustees seem intent on duplicating.

## PAY AND PERFORMANCE FOR COLLEGE LEADERS

In 2003, the Southern Region Education Board revealed that among colleges and universities in the South, inflation adjusted administrative salaries rose 22 percent over the five year period 1996–2001, while similarly adjusted faculty salaries rose just over 6 percent.[14]

Some have argued that management of universities today is a more complex work than it once was.[15] If true, however, is that increased complexity any more compelling for collegiate leaders than for those in complex public service endeavors such as government and military? What principle argues for a multi million dollar compensation package of a business executive, a million dollar compensation package for a college president while a four-star general may be commanding thousands of troops in a life and death business for a salary less than a quarter million?

In a board action of September 30, 2005, The Tennessee Board of Regents passed an action that would award presidents of campuses in that system salary increases of not less than 5 percent per year over the next three years. This action was justified on the distance between these Tennessee collegiate leaders and counterparts in other states, with the Chancellor of the Regents system commenting that the system did not want to lose its university heads over salaries. Indeed, perhaps someone should lose their heads if these presidents feel no shame in accepting 5 percent increases while their faculties received an average raise of 2percent in 2006–07.

The action was taken while faculties in that system and over the state had been experiencing relatively flat compensation profiles for over a decade. In the decade 1996–97 to 2005–06, the State of Tennessee appropriations for salary increases ranged from 0 percent in two years to 3.5 percent as maximum, with the average being approximately 2.5 percent. The average salary for all Tennessee faculties in 2001–02 was below the SREB average for southern states by approximately $43 million.[16] In 2001–02, the average deficit of Tennessee faculty salaries for four-year institutions compared to SREB four-year faculty salaries was approximately $600. By the 2004–05 year, that average deficit had grown to $3600, a major loss of position. Should the Tennessee Board of Regents have entertained a proposal to give its faculty and staff a guaranteed raise of 5 percent for each of three years, there is little doubt that the proposal would have been countered by the claim that no money was available. The availability of money for the presidential raises, however, seemed not to be a public issue.

The 2005 *Fact Book on Higher Education* published by the Southern Regional Education Board indicates that Tennessee was next to last among SREB states in percentage of salary increase over the ten years 1994–2004. The average salary increase for that period for the region was 9 percent, but for Tennessee faculty only 2 percent.[17]

The *Fact Book* reports that for this same period average salaries for administrators at four-year colleges in the South rose by 84 percent, gaining ground on national averages and in some cases surpassing national averages. The *Fact Book* concludes that: "Administrators' salaries tend to be closer to national averages than faculty salaries."[18]

As a passing and parenthetical aside on the matter of executive salaries, Jim Collins reported in his widely read book *Good to Great* that "We found no systematic pattern linking specific forms of executive compensation to the process of going from good to great. The idea that the structure of executive compensation is a key driver in corporate performance is simply not supported by the data."[19]

Earlier, in 2002, the University of Tennessee Board of Trustees appointed Dr. John Shumaker as president of the UT system, with a total salary package of approximately $750,000—at that time the second highest paid public college president in the nation—and produced a 200 percent increase in presidential salary inside of three years! Most faculty and staff would perform a jolly good dance should their salaries make such a percentage jump in three years! Did the University of Tennessee Trustees feel the same responsibility to care for the salary welfare of their faculty and staff as they did for the president? Did the unhappy symbolism of this move reach a level of awareness for board members? Apparently not.

We have argued for the importance of competent leadership in setting a climate for excellence and integrity for any college or university. But presidents alone do not produce academic success or excellence. As former Harvard University president Derek Bok wrote ". . . almost everything that matters in an institution–the quality of education, the creativity of the faculty, even the amount of money raised—is the work of so many hands that no one can be certain of the president's role in obtaining the final result."[20] This reflection encourages critical reflection on executive compensation for colleges and universities, just as the previously cited commentary from Jim Collins on executive compensation encourages critical reflection.

It is often argued that premier salaries are required to attract high quality university administrators. The influence of the market was cited as the reason University of Tennessee Board of Trustees paid John Shumaker $750,000 in salary when he was hired in 2001. Just two short years later, the Board of Trustees paid Dr. John Petersen $400,000 to do the same job—some $350,000 less than Shumaker. What a crazy market!! The complexity of the presidency could hardly have changed—or diminished—in that period of time! Boards of Trustees may be creating markets rather than responding to markets for college presidents.

The November 24, 2006, "Executive Compensation" section of *The Chronicle of Higher Education* featured on its front page public research university presidential salaries ranging from $277,491 for Shirley Raines at the University of Memphis to $974,571 for David P. Roselle at the University of Delaware.[21] Is there something about the marketplace that creates this difference? Stranger still, why would the president of a small private college of less than 1000 students, such as Kathleen Bowman at Randolph Macon, make close to $378,304 and Donald Ross of 2300-student Lynn University make close to $1,313,255 in annual compensation, both in dramatic contrast to public presidents responsible for larger and more complex enterprises in size, budget, and program? What a puzzling market!!

This same November 24, 2006, issue of the Chronicle carried a story entitled "The Million Dollar President, Soon to be Commonplace?" on journalistic and public scrutiny of high presidential salaries, reporting that over the previous year, there had been a 53 percent increase in presidents making more than $500,000.[22] Among the presidents profiled was Gordon Gee of Vanderbilt, whose million dollar salary and $700,000 expense account had been the subject of an article by Lublin and Golden in the September 26, 2006, issue of the *Wall Street Journal*.[23]

Of additional interest in the Wall Street Journal story were notes on Constance Gee, wife of President Gee and a professor of public policy and education at Vanderbilt. Apparently Ms. Gee had been using marijuana at the presidential mansion Braeburn—which had just undergone a $6 million renovation—and had lowered the flag in front of the presidential residence in liberal mourning when President Bush was re-elected in 2004. When confronted by board members on the issue of his wife using marijuana, Mr. Gee's response was that his wife smoked marijuana for an inner ear infection. This no doubt will prove a useful excuse for other culprits nailed by law enforcement for marijuana use and possession. Mr. Gee also reported that this was the first presidency in which he made more than the football coach. More on this comment at the end of this essay.

As a postscript, the Vanderbilt Board created a website responding to the *Wall Street Journal* story (http://www.vanderbilt.edu/news/wsj). The website presented an impressive profile of both academic and financial achievements under President Gee's leadership.

The July 7, 2006 issue of *The Chronicle of Higher Education* carried a front page story by Paul Fain[24] on the apparent suicide death of Dr. Denice Denton, chancellor of the University of California at Santa Clara. Apparently the suicide followed an intense period of criticism reaching over sixteen months that included widespread dissatisfaction with a range of matters, from compensation to personnel appointments. Nestled in the article was one item concerning a $30,000 dog run built for the chancellor's residence.

It is a challenge to guard one's reaction and language as we think about such an expenditure. One can only wonder what influences the value systems of campus leaders that renders them so insensitive to the public perceptions of such foolish use of public and private funds. Surely, a visit to Pet Smart or consultation with a capable fence builder could have produced a dog-friendly containment facility for much less; and perhaps the chancellor herself should have fronted this expenditure.

Now back to the matter at hand, presidential compensation. As earlier noted, one has to wonder whether the market is producing these escalating but conflicting presidential compensation packages or whether Boards of Trustees are creating a market. Once one college president is given a large salary increase, one can predict the pressure for other presidents, and one can predict the escalation of salaries for executive level administrations, vice presidents and deans, within an institution.

The market argument may be advanced for the recruitment of faculty. Ehrenberg has documented a link between salary and faculty turnover. Using 1988–89 American Association of University Professors (AAUP) salary data, his group found higher retention rates at institutions with higher average salaries, especially among doctoral/research universities.[25]

In the 1990s, the state of Georgia made a committed, four-year effort to raise faculty salaries if specific performance standards were met. The national reputation and ranking of Georgia institutions, notably the University of Georgia, have risen sharply in the wake of this commitment. This advancement was made possible by a united effort on the part of Georgia's governor Zell Miller, legislature, and higher education leadership. Nationally recognized academic leader and scholar Frank Newman, now deceased, noted in his book *Choosing Quality* that will and aspiration were central factors in the quality of a state higher education system: "Aspiration: The most important ingredient to have a university—and a system of higher education—of high quality."[26]

## THE ABANDONMENT OF INTEGRITY

Enough on the growing distance between the pay of those on the firing line and those in the power suite. Let's probe the performance and integrity of our corporate and collegiate leaders. The price of duplicity in any sector of our national life is mistrust and cynicism, incendiary outcomes dangerous to the health of a democracy. Who will pay in money and pain for the Enron mess, for sex offense scandals in the Catholic Church, for embezzlement and misappropriated dollars in government, for outrageous expenditures by executives of fund raising organizations such as United Way? Stockholders, employees, parishioners, taxpayers, beneficiaries! Men and women struggling to live on minimum wage, who have lost their jobs, their homes, their retirement savings in the twilight years of their lives are not impressed that one of these wayward corporate executives had to sell one of their several vacation homes. Nor are minimum wage staff serving at colleges and universities impressed that the executive mansion needs sprucing up or a new dog run.

On the matter of executive integrity, regrettably, we have had too many sad and similar examples in collegiate leadership, and some campus administrators seem intent on replicating the disappointing ethical behavior of corporate rascals. Within a year of taking office, President Shumaker of the University of Tennessee was invited to resign because of irregularities in spending habits and questionable use of the university airplane. He had over twenty phones installed in the presidential residence, enough to have one on each side of every commode in the presidential residence and most other rooms covered as well. Apparently in responding to the market, the Board of Trustees not only brought to the University a highly paid president but one with imperial style and dubious integrity.

"Shumaker audit embarrasses officials. Trustees negligent in giving UT president 'blank check' . . . " was the front page headline in *The Tennessean* on August 14, 2003.[27] This story appeared to have nasty roots of unending proportion, with charges of a "rigged" presidential search brought not by the state auditor but by Shumaker's former wife, these charges being aired in *The Chronicle of Higher Education* on August 15, 2003.[28]

Shumaker's derailment had been immediately preceded by the earlier June, 2001 non-voluntary departure of UT President Wade Gilley, who served less than two years and left amidst a sexual scandal featuring a front page public airing of spicy emails between Mr. Gilley and Pamela Reed, both of whom were married, but not to one another.[29]

Just two short years after he was employed as President of Middle Tennessee State University, President Sydney McPhee came under scrutiny by the Tennessee Board of Regents for charges of sexual harassment. He was fined $10,000 and placed on suspension from December 15, 2002, through January 3, 2003.[30] Since this was Christmas break, one supposes that the Board of Regents thought the university could make it through the holidays without McPhee supervising the empty campus. The poet Kahlil Gibran wrote, "I have learned silence from the talkative and tolerance from the intolerant; yet strange, I am ungrateful to these teachers."[31] Will our students learn good ethics lessons from bad presidential exemplars?

President James Hefner of Tennessee State University was directed to repay $9,800 to a scholarship fund for illegally accepting 2001 super bowl tickets and hotel expenses from a university vendor, this after Dr. Hefner originally lied to auditors about the tickets. The Tennessee Board of Regents' solution to this behavior was to propose the appointment of an executive vice president to oversee campus operations.[32] Scott Adams, author of the Dilbert cartoons, would have a field day thinking about this incredulous and expensive solution for promoting and insuring presidential honesty. I am not necessarily a big fan of Donald Trump but here are two cases where "You're fired!" would work.

What happens to seduce the vision, to sear the conscience, and to seal the empathy of officers in executive suites so that they take the men and women of their colleges and corporations and the customers/clients of those organizations in harm's way with behavior both duplicitous and arrogant? Most of those offending corporate executives hold degrees from our colleges and universities, as do the offending college presidents. Are we educating for technical competence but not for moral conscience in our colleges and universities?

What are the effects of trustee and administrative behaviors that are symbolically insensitive and ethically wrongheaded? The most immediate and insidious effect is a growing public mistrust and cynicism with all of our organizations—to say nothing of the financial losses and the loss of attention to duty occasioned by the distractions of dealing with duplicity made public. This cynicism will eventually beget a loss of trust and participation, a fearful and fatal outcome to the health of a democracy.

Thus, there is both ethical and practical justification for corporate and collegiate leaders to honor empathy and integrity and to honor the "role" call of the servant/exemplar leader. We do what is right because there is moral principle to commend it. We do what is right because we fear the reprisal and retribution of those whom we cheat of life and property. We do what is right because any act of ethical wrongdoing pollutes some economic, political or social reservoir.

If we fail to do what is right, beyond the earlier cited outcomes of cynicism and mistrust, there is a far more destructive cost that may be paid. A smoldering fire and rage may build beneath the social, political, and economic surface; and the future may be filled with the sound of high heels and wing tip shoes coming down the stairs and the thunder of work boots and tennis shoes racing up the stairs in a convulsion of social and economic justice. Writing in *Rules for Radicals*, Saul Alinsky observed that, "I believe that man is about to learn that the most practical life is the moral life and that the moral life is the only road to survival. He is beginning to learn he will either share part of his material wealth or lose all of it. . . . "[33]

Duplicity and arrogance in executive suites is not the commanding reality in either our colleges or our corporations. And so our sense of public optimism is not entirely extinguished when we consider the great majority of leaders exemplifying competence and conscience in their work every day. However, just one departure from nobility, just one collegiate leader who sacrifices his or her sense of honor is one too many.

Given that Alinksy's note " . . . the moral life is the only road to survival" was written over a quarter century ago, that income and wealth gaps between those in the executive suite and those on the firing line appear to be exacerbating in recent years, and that highly able but dishonest executives continue to take their organizations and people in harm's way, our optimism is surely getting a splendid test.

There is a saying that "You get what you pay for." What we may be paying for is million dollar college presidents sitting in executive stadium suites watching million dollar coaches perform while faculty/staff in classrooms and offices, and perhaps taxpayers, grow increasingly discontent and contentious with the growing inequity in college compensation profiles.

Those presidents and trustees who contribute to continuing gross pay inequities will be among those surprised when a future Saul Alinsky provides advice to folks in the trenches on how to discomfort those in the power suites. One might believe that colleges and universities would be immune to such wrenching social turmoil. There is little, however, in the current record to encourage the belief that college presidents and trustees are thinking about the meaning and implications of the leadership metaphors "servant" and "steward."

## NOTES

1. John Gardner, *On Leadership* (New York, NY: The Free Press, 1990), 67.

2. James Kouzes, and Barry Posner, *Credibility* (San Francisco, CA: Jossey-Bass Publishers, 1993), 14.

3. Sara Hebel, "Same Classroom, Different Price," *The Chronicle of Higher Education*, September 19, 2003, A10–A 11.

4. Scott McCartney, "Livid Over Executive Pay, AMR Unions May Balk at Cuts," *The Wall Street Journal*, April 18, 2003, B1.

5. Robert Greenleaf, *Servant Leadership* (New York, NY: Paulus Press, 1977).

6. John Gardner, *Excellence* (New York, NY: W. W. Norton, 1984), 107.

7. Robert Heilbroner and others, *In the Name of Profit* (New York, NY: Doubleday, 1972).

8. James Stewart, *Den of Thieves* (New York, NY: Simon and Schuster, 1991).

9. Arianna Huffington, *Pigs at the Trough* (New York, NY: Crown, 2003).

10. Kenneth Eichewald, *Conspiracy of Fools* (New York, NY: Broadway Books, 2005).

11. Andrew Tobias, "How Much Is Fair?" *Parade Magazine*, March 2, 2003, 10–11.

12. Alejandro Gonzalez, "Our View on CEO Compensation: When Failure's Worth $200M, Something's Out of Whack," *USA Today*, January 8, 2007.

13. Rachel Kovac, "State Income Gap Continues to Grow," *Knoxville News Sentinel*, January 27, 2006, B2–B3.

14. *SREB Fact Book on Higher Education* (Atlanta, GA: Southern Regional Education Board, 2003).

15. Donald Kennedy, *Academic Duty* (Cambridge, MA: Harvard University Press, 1997).

16. Russ Deaton, Tennessee Higher Education Commission, Nashville, Tennessee, email to author. 2006.

17. *SREB Fact Book on Higher Education*, 159.

18. Ibid., 161.

19. Jim Collins, *Good to Great* (New York, NY: Harper Business, 2001), 10.

20. Derek Bok, "Are Huge Presidential Salaries Bad for Colleges?" *The Chronicle of Higher Education*, November 22, 2002, B20.

21. "Executive Compensation: What Leaders Make," *The Chronicle of Higher Education*, November 24, 2006, B1.

22. "The Million Dollar President, Soon to Be Commonplace?" *The Chronicle of Higher Education*, November 24, 2006, B3.

23. Joann Lublin and Daniel Golden, "Golden Touch: Vanderbilt Reins in Lavish Spending by Star Chancellor," *Wall Street Journal*, September 28, 2006, A1.

24. Paul Fain, "In Apparent Suicide, Chancellor Dies in a Fall," *The Chronicle of Higher Education*, July 7, 2006, 1.

25. Ronald Ehrenberg, Hirschel Kasper, and Daniel Rees, "Faculty Turnover in American Colleges and Universities," *Economics of Education Reviews* 10, no. 2 (1991): 99–110.

26. Frank Newman, *Choosing Quality* (Denver, CO: Education Commission of the States, 1987), 87.

27. Michael Cass and Bonna de la Cruz, "Shumaker Audit Embarrasses Officials," *The Tennessean*, August 14, 2003, 1A, 2A.

28. Jeffrey Selingo, "President of U. of Tennessee is Accused of Getting Job through Rigged Search," *The Chronicle of Higher Education*, August 15, 2003, A29.

29. Julianne Basinger, "Release of Racy e-mail Prompts Resignation," *The Chronicle of Higher Education*, June 29, 2001, A26.

30. Michael Cass, "McPhee Penality: $10,000, Suspension," *The Tennessean*, December 6, 2003, 1.

31. Kahlil Gibran, *Sand and Foam* (New York, NY: Knopf, 1973), 58.

32. Julianne Basinger, "Tennessee State U Reins in its President," *The Chronicle of Higher Education*, April 30, 2004, A29.

33. Saul Alinsky, *Rules for Radicals* (New York, NY: Random House, 1971), 23.

# CHAPTER

## Fish, Books and Politics: Patience and Persistence Payoffs

*Ours is a difficult and exhilarating form of government—not for the faint of heart, not for the tidy-minded, and in these days of complexity not for the stupid. We need men and women who can bring to government the highest order of intellect, social motivations sturdy enough to pursue good purposes despite setbacks, and a resilience of spirit equal to the frustrations of public life.*
—John Gardner, *No Easy Victories*

In the fall of 1991, shortly after I accepted appointment as chancellor of Louisiana State University in Shreveport, the University Librarian Malcolm Parker came to visit me about a private library of some 200,000 volumes that might be donated to the University. He invited me to accompany him to the building housing the library and to meet the owner of the library.

A few days later we drove through downtown Shreveport and entered the parking lot of an abandoned train station in north Shreveport. The granite building had no doubt been grand in its day, but looked now slightly forlorn. We walked up to an imposing metal door in the front of the building and knocked. In a moment, a peep-hole shutter was opened; and we were given admission by Ms. Lois Curtis who was an assistant to the owner of the library, Mr. Sonny Noel. This was an experience a little like seeking entrance to Hernando's Hideaway, as popularized in an older song by that title.

### LIBRARIAN AND OLYMPIC CLASS WRESTLER

Books on American and English literature and biography filled shelves in every direction on the main floor. In a moment, Mr. Noel appeared and greeted us with a friendly smile and invited us to the second floor conference room, where the train master had kept his office. In this conference room were many volumes, some four and five hundred years old and many with rich illustrations and gilded pages. In the ensuing conversation, I learned that Mr. Noel was interested in donating his collection to the University, with an accompanying endowment that might approximate $10 million. There were two conditions. He would spend not one penny on bricks and mortar so we had to secure funds to build a new library. And he wanted the library named for his family.

While we were engaged in conversation, Ms. Curtis came up the stairs and placed a loaded 38 caliber pistol on the conference table in front of Mr. Noel, indicating that she was going to the bank to make a deposit and she thought he might like to have the pistol. With a twinkle and a touch of mischief in his eye, Mr. Noel said, "Dr. Bogue, you could not fail to notice that my library and this old train station are not located in the best part of the city. I like to start out even when I come through the door every morning, and this gun gives me an edge in doing so." I cannot remember whether I offered a very coherent reply, but did manage to acknowledge the importance of his judgment in the matter.

Of Mr. Noel I learned this. He had been an Olympic class wrestler in his youth, and even though he was now 80, I decided I would not want to tangle with him in combat as he looked lean and fit. I learned that he had no children and only his wife as survivor. I learned that Mr. Noel would fight political battles to the highest levels on points of principle and that one did not negotiate with Mr. Noel. Thus, the library was a "take-it-or-leave-it" deal.

Mr. Parker and I were of common mind that acquisition of the private library would be a highly complementary and notable addition to our University Library of approximately the same size and that the depository of rare and contemporary volumes on American and British literature could become an important research asset. Here began a journey of ten years to satisfy the two conditions of Mr. Noel's agreement to donate the library. This journey involved intriguing governance interactions and political influence of the most fascinating kind. It is a study in patience and persistence. As I noted earlier in these essays, these are underrated leadership attributes for any leader but certainly for those who furnish leadership in college and university settings.

## POLITICAL AND GOVERNANCE INTRIGUE

First to the matter of naming the University Library for the Noel family. It took three years, but I was eventually able to persuade the Louisiana State Board of Supervisors, the University's multi-campus governing board, to name the existing library the Noel Memorial Library. I hauled gilded volumes up and down the highway to board meetings, had the President, board members, and other officers of the LSU system visit the library; and I engaged in other lobbying efforts to set this first step in place. The naming was not without serious policy complexity. In Louisiana, the policy for naming a public building was that buildings could not be named for any living party.

There is good sense in this policy, as it avoids the possibility that a person for whom a building is to be named might later embarrass the university with shady behavior. There are sad chronicles that might be offered by other institutions having erected a building in honor of a person, only to see the person honored later travel troubled public paths of moral and behavioral distortion of the first order. In this instance I made the case that the building was not being named for Mr. Noel, who obviously was still living, but for his family.

At the same time, I requested that the LSU Board of Supervisors forward a capital outlay request to the legislature and governor for planning and construction of the library. Here a short diversion is needed to describe the capital outlay and building approval process. The project had first to be approved by the LSU Board, which it was. The project was then forwarded to the Louisiana Board of Regents, a regulatory coordinating board for all public colleges and universities in the state. The Board of Regents then forwarded each year a prioritized list of capital projects for all colleges to the governor and legislature. Projects were approved in two steps. One had first to acquire money for planning and then money for construction.

Even with the "show and tell" approach of having lay members and staff of the Board of Regents view the rare and beautiful books typifying the collection, I was unable to advance the priority of the library project in the Regents listing. We were in 1986 able to get the legislature and governor to approve a little over $1 million for planning the library. Not, however, without an interesting event. When the project was under debate in the Senate, one member of the LSU Board of Supervisors went on the floor lobbying against the project—this after the LSU board had approved the project! Learning of the board member's action, I asked another member of the LSU Board from Shreveport to counter the negative lobbying effort and to make clear to senators that the project had been formally and officially approved by the LSU Board. The Shreveport Board member was a person of no small influence and public esteem, and possessed of happy lobbying skills. We got the planning money.

The design and architectural contract was given to the Shreveport firm of Demopolis and Associates. Within a year or more, we had plans for an imposing and beautiful new library building to grace the front of the campus, which was located on a major north-south highway running from Shreveport to Alexandria and thence to Baton Rouge.

## THE CULTIVATION OF INFLUENCE

How to take the next step, the acquisition of construction money for this $12 million project? Here we introduce another and important actor in this process. One of the members of the community I got to know by having breakfast and lunch one-on-one with civic leaders was a gentleman named Gus Majalis. Having lunch one day with a prominent banker in the city, I asked him to give me the names of two or three other folks that I should get to know in the city. As noted in an earlier essay, this networking allowed me to meet a wide variety of influential persons in the city, some holding formal corporate, business, and civic appointment and others holding no formal position but nevertheless having major voice and influence in the city.

On this particular day, the banker looked across the restaurant and pointed to a large man at a table and said to me, "Grady, if Edwin Edwards is elected to his third term as Governor in this state, that man you are looking at will become the second most powerful and politically influential man in this state. You should get to know him." And I did.

Gus Majalis was a man of formidable physique and Greek heritage who owned several fish markets in the city. To support his business, Gus had borrowed a large sum of money on a hand-written loan note from Mr. Sonny Noel, the potential donor of the private library. I had shared with Mr. Majalis our interest in building the library, and it would be fair to say that Mr. Majalis had good and personal reasons in being supportive of Mr. Noel's aspirations and hopes. While perhaps many socially active folks in Shreveport society would not describe either Mr. Noel or Mr. Majalis among the social elite of the city, there was nevertheless in their association a pleasant leverage that would yield positive political action as follows.

Edwin Edwards did win his third term as Governor and appointed Mr. Majalis as a member of the Louisiana Board of the Regents, the aforementioned coordinating board for higher education in the state.

In 1989, some eight to nine years after setting this journey in motion, the political and governance stars all fell into alignment. I was able to get the building in the legislative capital budget for construction with the assistance of a long term, well-respected state senator from Shreveport, Mr. Sydney Nelson. The Noel Library building request went into the capital outlay committee of the Board of Regents well down the priority list, not in the top ten projects. However, Mr. Majalis had become chairman of the facilities committee, and the Noel Library project emerged as number one on the priority list! Thus, we had the top recommendation of the Board of Regents and the building was in the legislative capital projects list. Only the governor remained to be persuaded.

Meanwhile Buddy Roemer had become governor. Buddy was from the Shreveport area, and I had invited him to be commencement speaker at LSU-Shreveport before he began his formal run for governor. We also had a former faculty member serving on the governor's staff. I called and talked to the staff member, indicating that we had the building first on the Regent's priority list of capital project and in the Legislative bill. He asked if we had someone knowledgeable of libraries that could give us a letter of evaluation to be sent to the governor. I did.

Dr. Edward Holly was then serving as an endowed professor of library and information sciences at the University of North Carolina and had served as university librarian at the University of Houston. I had become acquainted with Ed in earlier years of service with the Tennessee Higher Education Commission, using him as a consultant. I invited Ed to be a consultant in evaluating the Noel Library. He spent two days on campus and with the Noel collection, furnishing us a letter outlining the research value of the collection and valuing the collection itself at close to $4 million dollars, independent of the endowment to accompany.

This letter I immediately sent via Federal Express to the governor, suggesting that this was a win-win political act on his part, since both the Board of Regents and the Legislature had approved; and it would also be a chance to invest more than $10 million in the economy of the Shreveport area, which was in the economic doldrums at the time. He signed the bill, and the appropriation was formalized and finalized. In 1994, three years after I had departed the chancellor's position at LSUS to take professorial appointment at the University of Tennessee, I attended the dedication ceremony as guest of the university.

As noted news commentator Paul Harvey urged, we should hear "the rest of the story." Mr. Majalis was an adept political supporter of the University and clearly a major influence in helping us acquire the construction funds for the library. While Gus never asked me to take any step that was ethically questionable while I served as chancellor, apparently not all of his business involvements were without ethical blemish. Gus had also started a bank in Shreveport and in a few years the bank went out of business. More on the demise of his bank in a moment.

In the spring of 1990, after serving LSU Shreveport as chancellor for ten years (with one year away in 1989 to serve as interim chancellor of LSU Baton Rouge), I came to the conclusion that it was time for renewal for both me and the University. Moreover, we had three small children, all born in Shreveport, that were getting ready to enter their teen years; and I wanted to be able to spend time with them.

I resigned as chancellor of LSU Shreveport and gave the Board a year to find a replacement. I received honorable discharge from the LSU Board of Supervisors and was designated chancellor emeritus. In the summer of 1991, I accepted appointment as professor at the University of Tennessee Knoxville; and my wife and I moved back to our home state. We had met and loved many wonderful people in Louisiana and retain fond memories of our life in Shreveport and our service to LSU. One of those legacy memories is the beautiful Noel Library, the culmination of a decade's journey.

Now for the rest of the story. One summer day a few years after I had taken appointment at the University of Tennessee-Knoxville, I was sitting on my back deck, enjoying an afternoon of reading. The mobile phone rang and when I picked up, I heard the voice on the other end say "Grady, is that you, boy?" I knew immediately that it was Gus. The essence of his call was that Gus had been found guilty of improper operations in his Shreveport Bank and was about to go to federal prison. After explaining where he had been and where he was going, Gus asked, "Grady, is there any way you can write a letter to the federal judge that says anything nice about me?"

As I earlier reported, Gus had never asked me to be involved in any act illegal or unethical. And he had been a primary influence and force in our acquiring both planning and construction funds for the Noel Library, thus making both an economic and physical contribution to the University and to the community. And that's what I put in the letter to the federal judge. Gus served time in a low security federal prison.

## PATIENCE AND PERSISTENCE AS PREMIER LEADERSHIP VIRTUES

Of the several important values that should be honored in the lives of leaders, and especially collegiate leaders is persistence—the will, the patience, the determination, the resilience to pursue worthy goals over the long haul. Ray Kroc, the former president and founder of McDonald's is reputed to have said that "Nothing in the world can take the place of persistence. Talent will not; nothing is more common than unsuccessful men with great talent. Genius will not; unrewarded genius is almost a proverb. Education will not; the world is full of educated derelicts. Persistence and determination alone are omnipotent."

In a novel published in 1969, novelist Jan Westcott carried these lines of dialogue in *The White Rose*: "Patience, my boy. Patience is one of the virtues difficult to learn and so deadly when employed."[1] In no organization can patience and persistence be more powerful than in the leadership of colleges and universities. Colleges and universities often move at a glacial pace when it comes to change, a matter of some chagrin to corporate managers used to giving orders and having them followed. Collegiate leaders who hope to orchestrate a quick fix in any matter of policy or program may find that swift adoption is often followed by equally swift dissolution, especially if the change is insured by the constant thumb and authority pressure of an administrator.

Robert Hutchins, former president of the University of Chicago—rightly respected and quoted as one of the foremost scholars and practitioners in the history of American higher education—brought the "Great Books" curriculum to the University of Chicago. Within a short time of his departure from the presidency, however, the great books curriculum was also gone. Perhaps one reason is that the faculty did not feel any allegiance to that curriculum.

There is a corollary idea that should be considered here, the idea of ambition. The ambition to serve others may be properly distinguished from the ambition to serve self. Some collegiate leaders become afflicted with the idea that mobility and climbing the administrative status ladder—from director to dean, from provost to president—is the path to effectiveness.

When Dale Lick, former President of the University of Maine and Georgia Southern University, was appointed president of Florida State University, he looked at the presidency of Michigan State University, some say before his chair was warm at Florida State. Apparently Lick had not advised his system head, Florida System Chancellor Charles Reed; and Lick was invited to vacate the presidential chair at Florida State.[2]

Dr. John Darling succeeded me as chancellor of Louisiana State University in Shreveport. Within the first year, he was known to have been a presidential candidate at other universities. Might we conclude that he had come to invest in and serve LSU Shreveport? Hardly! Not surprisingly, president of the LSU system, Alan Copping, encouraged an early departure.

### OTHER VENTURES IN PERSISTENCE

The building of the Noel Library was one of several long-term achievements stretching over a ten year period. The second was movement of the University into a small college intercollegiate athletics program. When I arrived at LSU Shreveport, I was beneficiary of leadership and faculty commitment to high quality teaching, and the university held reputation for caring and competent teaching in the metropolitan community and over the state. We were missing, however, the emotional heart of an educational institution without major investment in music and athletics.

I tried to persuade the faculty to approve a small college intercollegiate athletics program but was unsuccessful for some obvious reasons. We were suffering through year after year of budget cuts occasioned by the dramatic decline in oil prices. The suggestion to implement even a small college intercollegiate athletics program led many faculty to think, with some justification perhaps, that not all my mental screws were in tight. My hope, however, was that the program could be supported by a dedicated student fee and that later we would attract community financial backing. I was convinced as well that small college intercollegiate athletics, well managed, would furnish another learning opportunity for our students and help us build additional connections with the community. The intercollegiate models I had in mind were not Ohio State University or The University of Michigan but Austin College in Texas and Maryville College in Tennessee. The second reason, and a legitimate one, was the faculty concern about the pressure for bracket creep, beginning with a small college NCAA III or NAIA program and then experiencing in short order the temptation to go big time. Thus, the proposal was not approved during the early years of my service as chancellor.

Upon returning from my tour of duty as interim chancellor of LSU Baton Rouge in late 1989, where I had an up close and personal look at big time athletics, I returned to the faculty with the proposal again. I publicly pledged that the program would not be implemented unless students were willing to vote a fee to pay for it, even though students had not been offered the option to approve other services for which their fees were used.

For reasons that to this day I am not sure I understand, the proposal for a small college program was approved without dissenting vote by the Faculty Council. Following the vote, I walked back across campus with one of our senior and well regarded professors, Dr. Ann Torrans. Ann was a lady of formidable physique, topping my 5'11" height by several inches. As we strolled down the main walk, Ann looked down at me and said, "Chancellor, do you know why I voted for that athletics proposal today?"

"Ann," I replied, "I hope you voted for it because you thought it was a correct program investment for the university to make in its students."

"Nope!" she quickly retorted. "The only reason I voted for that proposal was that I knew you would just keep dragging it back in the door until we did approve it."

I've been away fifteen years as I write these lines, and the athletics program is still there and flourishing as an NAIA program, with two of the teams—men's baseball and women's basketball—performing well in recent national NAIA competition. Able and sustained leadership by current Chancellor Vincent Marsala has been important to the program and other programs of the University.

Another long term venture was the creation of a four-station, public radio network. When I arrived on campus in 1980, there was an informal conversation running between University and community leaders on building a public radio station. While serving with the Tennessee Higher Education Commission in Tennessee, I had the opportunity to work with Dr. Don Mullaly from the University of Illinois in a study of public radio stations in Tennessee; and I invited Don down for consultation. We were able to secure leadership of Mr. Tom Livingston as the first manager; and he in turn orchestrated the acquisition of both public and private grants to build the first station. Station KDAQ went on the air in 1984 and was featured as a public service outreach of LSU Shreveport.

Tom did not stop there, and we subsequently opened three additional stations in two-year increments, including one station in Alexandria, one in southern Arkansas, and one in eastern Texas. The four stations serve a listening market of close to 3 million people and make an affirming cultural contribution to the life of the area.

When I arrived at the university in 1980, there was little or no private fund raising taking place. I employed Dr. Peter Smits, now Vice President for Advancement at California State University in Fresno, in the advancement and development position and we set about creating a foundation and raising private money.

In retrospect, I was working from a seriously flawed theory. For the first five years, my theory was that if I loved the community, the community would love the university financially and give money. And so I served on the Chamber of Commerce Board, the Symphony Board, the Boy Scout Council Board, the Red Cross Board, and in numerous civic capacities. What I failed to realize was that fund raising was an imminently personal work, requiring networking and personal cultivation. Nevertheless, over a period of ten years, we were able to set in place the foundation for private giving and began to attract support for scholarships and endowed professorships. Dr. Vincent Marsala, currently serving as LSU-S chancellor, has been highly successful in bringing exponential growth to private endowments, multiplying scholarship funds and the number of endowed chairs and professorships.

A final area of long term cultivation and achievement resided in the fiscal integrity of the University. While we had the unhappy experience of going through many years of difficult budgets flowing primarily from downturn in oil prices and subsequent negative impact on state government revenues, we were nevertheless able to manage our finances with fiscal integrity.

During the ten years I served as chancellor, we did not receive a single fiscal audit exception in our yearly audits by state government auditors. While this was a pleasant achievement, it carried a distinctly uncomfortable outcome, as the state auditors would come to our campus for training The fiscal management achievement of the University I can attribute directly to the talent and integrity of two serving as vice chancellor for Business Affairs in my term of service, Dr. A.J. Howell and Ms. Fabia Thomas, and to the good work of their directors and staffs.

## UNDERRATED VIRTUES AND COLORFUL POLITICAL PARTNERS

There are two leadership lessons flowing from these reflections. First, leaders in any enterprise, and no less so in collegiate enterprise, are called upon to work with a wide range of personalities and behavioral dispositions. Both former Governor Edwin Edwards and Mr. Gus Majalis have served time in federal prisons. I worked successfully with both of them, but my relationships with them did not require sacrifice of either personal or public integrity. And I was grateful for the good work made possible by their support.

The story is told that so committed was Winston Churchill to the defeat of Hitler in World War II that if Hitler were to invade Hell, he (Mr. Churchill) would be willing to make a passing favorable reference to the Devil in Parliament. Well, I did not have to consort with the Devil, but I did get to work with some colorful personalities. More importantly, I derived much pleasure in working with a diverse array of other Shreveport and state citizens that included civic, professional, and corporate leaders.

Second, as well regarded military/government leader and scholar John Gardner noted in the quote opening this chapter, leadership in governmental enterprise is not for the faint hearted or tidy minded. Surely, this is the case for collegiate leaders who are not likely to realize constructive and long standing policy, program, or facility improvements without discovering the power of persistence and patience, resilience, and determination.

## NOTES

1. Jan Westcott, *The White Rose* (New York, NY: G. P. Putnam's Sons, 1969), 284.

2. Courtney Leatherman, "Breach of Etiquette Costs President of Florida State U His Job," *Chronicle of Higher Education*, September 1, 1993, A21.

# CHAPTER

# Leadership Reveille: Open Heart Realities and Leadership Style

*Style is merely a consequence of what we believe, of what is in our hearts.*
— Max Depree, *Leadership is An Art*

*We share responsibility for creating the external world by projecting a spirit of light or a spirit of shadow on that which is other than us. Either a spirit of hope or a spirit of despair.*
— Parker Palmer, *Leading from Within*

Mid way in my ten-year tenure as chancellor of LSU Shreveport in the mid 1980s, we had convened a meeting of the LSUS Foundation Board, a fund raising and advancement organization for the University. Director of Development Dr. Peter Smits had led the way in designing the bylaws for the new foundation, in working with civic leaders in support of the foundation, and in securing approval from the LSU Board of Supervisors, the University's governing board.

Nestled among larger agenda items for the day, I casually mentioned that I was trying to find $30,000 to acquire new desktop computers for our computer science faculty. The next morning I was in a cheerful early morning mood as I sat eating breakfast and reading the morning paper around 6:00 AM. More on the origins of this early morning disposition in my life in a moment.

The phone in the kitchen rang a moment after 6:00 AM, and when I picked it up with a friendly "Hello," I heard the voice of foundation chairman John Turk, who was also President/CEO of our regional utility Southwestern Electric Power Company (SWEPCO). "Grady, Boy," John said, as though it were middle of the day and business as usual, "If you thought you could come by my office today between 10:00 o'clock and noon, I might be able to find that $30,000 you said you needed for those computers."

"John," I replied, "I'm sure I can get by, and I'll look forward to seeing you then."

I did make it downtown to SWEPCO corporate offices, and I did bring back to the University a check for $30,000. Governor, mayor, chamber president, college chancellor, General Motors plant manager, city councilman—John had developed the reputation for making contact with a range of civic leaders early in the morning.

A few years later, as John was getting ready to retire, I made a personal and special trip downtown to express appreciation for his civic investment in the community and his special support of the University. It was in the middle of the summer, and temperatures had been hovering around 100 degrees for several days. When I was ushered into John's office, he was standing behind his desk watching a power meter on his office credenza hum away, a meter indicating how much power was being consumed in the SWEPCO service area at that moment.

As I walked in, I said "John, are you making some money today?"

"Awe, Grady, I just hope folks can pay for what they're using, cause they're using a whopping lot of power," he responded.

John was not an unusually tall man, but did have a commanding physical presence, a presence complemented by an immediately attracting and warm Texas personality, John having family heritage from the Lone Star state. He had indeed invested his talent and caring in civic and community ventures upon coming to Shreveport and would leave behind a grateful community.

I expressed my appreciation to John for that community gift and also expressed appreciation for his time spent in leadership of the University foundation and for his personal and corporate generosity. And then I said, "John, we are really going to miss you around the city. Not only are we going to miss your good spirit and generosity, I don't know who we are going to get to call us up to do business so early in the morning," a friendly salute to his disposition to call folks great and small in status before the rooster had crowed on most mornings.

With a big Texas grin, John replied, "Grady, you'd be surprised how many folks you can catch at home that time of day." Well, I had no doubt that what John said was true; and though I am an early morning person, I never cultivated the early phone call style that John deployed so well. He will be remembered for his leadership style and effectiveness.

## IN THE MORNING TIME

Here may be a good place to talk briefly about the morning time in my life. I'm not altogether sure when my love of the quietness and sunrise beauty of the morning began. I am sure it did not begin with my farmer dad pulling me out of bed at 4:30 AM in summer mornings when I was a teenager so that we could be in the cotton fields in the Mississippi River bottoms by 6:00 AM. In the bumpy drive to the bottoms farmland in our 1948 Chevy truck, I concluded that the only possible entity awake and conscious that time of day was God.

Somewhere between those reluctant early morning farm ventures and college, however, I developed a love of the morning. I was widely reviled by my college residence hall mates for singing in the shower at 7:00 AM in the morning. Had stones been available, I am sure my hall mates would have launched at me as though they were trying to hush some mockingbird singing lustily on the rooftop in the early morning.

Perhaps I can recall when the morning became a serious matter. Upon graduation from college, I entered active duty as a lieutenant with the air force. While I had completed a preflight program as an air force ROTC cadet and anticipated entering flight training, I failed the flight physical upon entering active duty and was sent to electronics maintenance school at Keesler Air Force Base, with a learning venture there reported earlier in Chapter 3. After a year's study of radar and computer electronics, I was ordered to Alaska where I became the electronics maintenance officer for a remote and isolated radar site hosting some 300 men. My first duty morning, I went to the dining hall and thence into the smaller dining room set aside for the dozen or so officers on the site. There I sat down to a hearty breakfast of hot coffee and a breakfast concoction affectionately known by military personnel as "SOS." A generous rendering of cream beef over toast will give the uninitiated reader some clue to the meaning of the acronym. And if you can't figure it out or find a friend with military background, give me a phone call or email.

In a moment, I was joined across the table by a captain from the radar operations section and shortly thereafter by the new commander of the site, a lieutenant colonel who sat at the head of the dining table. He looked at me and the captain and remarked, "Well, I can tell who my really good officers are by those who are up and moving in the morning." The next day, a dozen officers were sitting around the breakfast table at 6:00 AM!

## OF LEADERSHIP STYLE, PERSONALITY, AND TRAITS

Earlier, I stated that John Turk, the CEO of SWEPCO would be positively remembered for his leadership style and effectiveness. Recently a large university president in Tennessee was described as "imperial" and a small, private college president as "intimidating," with remembrances of their style being less flattering. Now these two adjectives don't say much about their outward appearance, but they do convey something about the perceived values of these two presidents. Exactly what do we mean by the term "style"? Leadership style is one of those terms often used in organizational conversation, but like terms such as quality and accountability, there may be more assumed understanding than really exists. Is style a matter of personality, a matter of behavior, a matter of values?

Research on leadership style has its origins in the 1950s and 1960s, where researchers uncovered leadership dispositions for task orientation and person orientation, the two-factor theories of style. The Ohio State studies of John Hemphill and Alvin Coons led in the study of leadership style, with "task orientation" centering on completion of task and the "relationship orientation" accenting group cohesiveness.[1] The two-factor concept was later popularized in a widely circulated book by Robert Blake and Jane Mouton (1964) entitled *The Managerial Grid*. A note in the preface of that book is revealing when the authors comment that "Students of management theory and management training . . . decided that management is a science rather than an art, and that it can be learned."[2] Here I would like to refer the reader to Chapter 3 where I spoke of the knowledge of practice. We can learn both science and art.

What had emerged in the early years of the 20th century was the "scientific management" approach to leadership, often traced to the writings of Frederick Winslow Taylor,[3] and concentrating on worker efficiency and productivity. Scholars of leadership might have been viewed as human and process engineers, exploring the environmental and process variables that offered promise of enhancing production.

The "human relations" approach to leadership, often traced to the writings of Elton Mayo[4] and the now famous Hawthorne studies, revealed that employee satisfaction, motivation, and productivity could be traced as quickly to such variables as caring and reinforcement as to physical variables thought to affect productivity.

Here we might reflect on a work cited earlier in these essays, the book *Reframing Organizations* by Lee Bolman and Terrence Deal,[5] which is one of the better volumes integrating a wide range of research and thought on leadership and organizational behavior. In addition to its suggestion that we may gain a more comprehensive view of the multiple truths of any organization by viewing the organization through four frames—the structural, the human relations, the political, and the symbolic—the book may be read as a narrative of how our understandings of leadership have unfolded. Structural views are more closely associated, for example, with the aforementioned scientific management school of thought, whereas the human relations views center more on topics under discussion here, the topic of style.

Later, other scholars expanded on the two-factor theory of leadership style. Leader relationships with different group expectations were featured in Fred Fielder's *A Theory of Leadership Effectiveness*,[6] and leader relationship with followers was featured in such works as Paul Hersey's *The Situational Leader*.[7] In his book *Managerial Effectiveness*, W. J. Reddin[8] continued the research dialogue, accenting the contingency concept. In contingency theory, style is adjusted to account for a third variable such as group expectations and leader-follower relationships.

Is "leadership style" therefore a matter of our inclination to focus on task or on relationship and adjust to contingencies in the environment, or is it more complicated than that? Clearly, this early research revealed inclinations or dispositions toward task or relationship. Are there other "inclinations" that might be a part of style? Here perhaps we should mention the research on personality type popularized by Myers-Brigg and operationalized in the Myers Brigg Type Indicator. Four dimensions of personality preference are conceptualized along four continua linking our inclinations to "Extroversion versus Introversion,

Thinking versus Feeling, Sensing versus Intuition, and Judgment versus Perception." See the book *Gifts Differing* by Isabel Myers.[9]

Style, then, engages questions of how leaders array their behavior on a number of variables: whether they tend to authoritarian/autocratic behaviors or
democratic/egalitarian behaviors, whether they tend to be directive in decision
making or more inclusive and participative, whether they tend to be more
closed and restricted in communication/information sharing or more candid
and open in communication, whether they tend to use threats or rewards as
motivational tools, whether they tend to treat subordinates with trust or suspicion.

In his work *The Human Organization*, Rensis Likert[10] presented an instrument
for the assessment of management "systems" that considered the leadership culture of an organization on the previously mentioned variables. Readers interested in a more extensive exploration of leadership style may find that in Bernard Bass's book *Handbook of Leadership Theory, Research, and Managerial
Applications*[11] and in the summary volume on leadership style by Lin Bothwell.[12]

Well, then, is leadership style descriptive of these behavioral inclinations on
how we work with others or might it include other factors such as John Turk's
practice of calling folks early in the morning, certainly a memorable dimension
of John's leadership and personality. Well, let's return for a moment to John
Turk. John was his own man, a man of affectionate personality and generous
physique, both wrapped around a quick mind and caring heart.

For years, leadership researchers looked for common traits among leaders and
ended up with a list that sounded like a good boy scout. We should acknowledge that much of the research in those early years was done by males with
male subjects. Basically, what they found is that there is no attribute profile
that describes every effective leader. This, however, has not kept us from exploring those factors of intellect, personality, and physique that might point us
to folks who are potentially good leaders. If the reader will be patient with an
extended quote, Peter Drucker summed up science and experience when he
wrote in his 1966 work *The Effective Executive* as follows:

> Among the effective executives I have known and worked with, there are extra-
> verts and aloof retiring men, some even morbidly shy. Some are eccentrics, oth-
> ers painfully correct conformists. Some are fat and some are lean. Some are worri-
> ers, and some are relaxed. Some drink quite heavily, others are total abstainers.
> Some are men of great charm and warmth, some have no more personality than
> a frozen mackerel. . . . Among the effective executives I have met, there are peo-
> ple who use logic and analysis and others who rely mainly on perception and
> intuition. There are men who make decisions easily and men who suffer agonies
> every time they have to move.[13]

In a more recent work *Good to Great*, researcher Jim Collins[14] found that
executives in companies that had moved to a sustaining leadership position in
their respective corporate fields were what he described as Level 5 leaders,
possessed of humility and strong determination. In a partial affirmation, Har-

vard scholar Joseph Badarracco wrote in his book *Leading Quietly* about quiet leaders as follows: "They move patiently, carefully, and incrementally. They do what is right—for their organizations, for the people around them, and for themselves—inconspicuously and without casualties."[15]

In sharp contrast is an earlier work entitled *An Anatomy of Leadership: Princes, Heros, and Supermen* by Eugene Jennings (1960). In his opening Acknowledgment section, Jennings advances the conviction that "Conspicuous personality is a requirement of great leadership."[16]

So is leadership style about being a heroic figure or a quiet figure? Is it about being humble or assertive? Is it about history and events making the great leader or is it about the leader making history and great events? Is it about being power driven or purpose driven? Is it about meeting the expectations of others or the expectations of self? Is it about being a General George Patton or a General Omar Bradley, a General Dwight Eisenhower or General Douglas McArthur? Is it about former Hewlett Packard CEO Carly Fiorina or former Prime Minister of Great Britain Margaret Thatcher? Is it about former Notre Dame president Theodore Hesburg or former Boston University president John Silber? Is it about former University of Chicago president Hannah Arendt or former California State University President Ann Reynolds?

Surely, intelligence and energy are central to effective leadership in any enterprise. If we use the more conventional definition of intelligence, the big "I," then what we discover is that some leaders can be smart and dumb at the same time, as I have already commented on that in earlier chapters. The research of Robert Sternberg (*The Triarchic Mind*),[17] Howard Gardner (*Frames of Mind: The Theory of Multiple Intelligence*),[18] and Daniel Golman (*Emotional Intelligence*)[19] have shown that perhaps there are many forms of intelligence that may include an ability to work with ideas and another ability to work with people and in applied settings. Gardner posits verbal, analytical, interpersonal, musical, psychomotor intelligence; and Goleman explores such matters as managing anger and personal gratification and exhibiting empathy.

The research work on leadership attributes, style, and personality, notwithstanding, some still hold to informal assumptions and theories on leadership effectiveness attributes:

- Leaders are handsome/beautiful.
- Leaders are tall.
- Leaders come to the office early and leave late.
- Leaders take work (or left over sandwiches) home in their briefcase.
- Leaders arrive at meetings late and leave early, signals of their busyness.
- Leaders use gadgets and the latest in electronic devices.
- Leaders keep pictures of themselves with prominent political figures.
- Leaders are assertive/take-charge personalities.

Whether these pseudo indicators align with effectiveness seems not to concern us when we are making decisions about selection or performance. We can add to this list other prejudicial attitudes often found in the academy such as: "We need someone grounded in the liberal arts." Or "What can you expect from someone with a degree from a cow and plow palace like A & M?" Or "How can this candidate lead a major research university without having served in one?"

Those looking for a profile of personality characteristics may be looking for an easy path of leadership advancement or perhaps some guarantee of leadership recognition and selection. If I look like a leader or have the personality of a leader, I will be a leader. Ralph Waldo Emerson warned of the danger here, however, in a lovely line from his essay *An Address:* "Imitation cannot go above its model. The imitator dooms himself to hopeless mediocrity."[20]

So apparently there are few if any personality traits that help us identify a promising and/or effective leader, and there are serious complications in finding a stylistic inclination that is effective in all situations. There are two applied benefits that have emerged from the research. One centers on the importance of self knowledge. For example, I know that I am first inclined to task orientation rather than relationship orientation and that I am an "ENTJ" Myers-Brigg type. The major contribution of the research is to understand that those who exemplify other styles and personality preferences are not "wrong" but different.

As important is the ability and the willingness to adjust style to policy, person, and place, there are moments for telling and moments for inquiring. There are moments for gentleness and moments for hard-nosed behavior. There are moments for trust and moments for audits. There are moments for persuasion and moments for threat. In Chapter 2, I argued for leadership as an art form, as have other writers and scholars. Knowledge and adaptability are central to the art.

## OPEN HEART REALITIES AND LEADERSHIP STYLE

Well, then, what do we know at the end of the day about leadership style and its relationship to effectiveness. In Chapter 11 we will speak of differential tests of leadership effectiveness, with goal and mission achievement perhaps preeminent among those indicators of effectiveness. Obviously many different styles can be effective in goal and mission achievement. Let me advance my conviction on style this way. Style is a term we use to embrace and to describe a cluster of physical/personality attributes, behavioral inclinations, and value dispositions.

As I move to closing reflections, let me mention one other style exemplar. Dr. Archie Dykes has been a mentor and friend over the past forty years in my life. In the 1960s, as one of my graduate professors, he encouraged me in doctoral work. Archie subsequently served as chancellor of three different universities: The University of Tennessee at Martin, The University of Tennessee at Knoxville, and for eight years at The University of Kansas. He later served as CEO of Security Benefit Insurance Company for several years, one of the nation's largest insurance companies; and he has served on several corporate boards.

Archie is not a tall man nor possessed of unusual or imposing physique; and I am quite convinced that he never worried about any of these attributes or what he should have printed on his business and calling card. Here's what he did have. His "style" included a well balanced concern for goal and a capacity to be personal. Once Archie had met you, you could depend on a friendly letter following within a day or two. He moved about his organizations encouraging and inspiring folks, again exemplifying that capacity to be personal. He was inspiring both as teacher and administrator. Once exposed to his energy, curiosity, and caring, one was ashamed not to be giving his or her best.

He had what some might consider a pedestrian set of educational credentials, a B.S. from East Tennessee State University and an Ed. D. from the University of Tennessee at Knoxville. His commitment, however, was to performance and competence, not pedigree and appearance; and that commitment along with his extraordinary interpersonal intelligence enabled him to give leadership in both colleges and corporations. He married courage with a caring for person and principle. Throughout the forty years of our acquaintance, I have learned to expect at any time a friendly phone call, email, or letter inquiring as to how I am doing.

What made the leadership styles of John Turk and Archie Dykes memorable? Well John's style was surely marked by that inclination to call you early in the morning and Archie's style by his extraordinary personal touch and communication. But their styles were more than that.

One of the quotes opening this chapter is Max Depree's observation that "Style is merely a consequence of what we believe, of what is in our hearts."[21] So what was in John Turk's heart? First was a keen sense of civic caring and desire to serve. And if I am to judge his corporate heart from those who worked with and for John, I would say that he honored the values of civility and candor in his work as CEO of SWEPCO. And what was in Archie Dykes' heart? Carried in his heart was the desire to encourage the promise of those entrusted to his care and a duty to integrity, a drive to do what was right. In the lives of both these leaders, the inside lived on the outside! And so it was with the two presidents previously described as imperial and intimidating.

Corporate and collegiate leaders may call folks before the break of dawn or write frequent personal notes/letters, drive a pick-up truck or a Buick to work, wear bow ties or conservative dresses, escape to a mountain cabin for a month or take no vacation, play golf or the cello, read mystery novels or physics texts, collect rocks or antique recordings. These habits may make our leaders colorful and memorable. It is, however, what Bellah[22] calls "the habits of heart," the values they exemplify, that are the primary expressions of style when it comes to leadership effectiveness. Open heart realities are what folks see in our style, our values at work in public forum.

## NOTES

1. John Hemphill, J. and Alvin Coons, "Development of the Leader Behavior Description and Questionnaire," in *Leader Behavior: Its Description and Measurement* (Mono-

*graph* 88), ed. R. M. Stogdill and A. E. Coons (Columbus, OH: Bureau of Business Research, Ohio State University, 1957).

2. Robert Blake and Jane Mouton, *The Managerial Grid* (Houston, TX: Gulf Publishing Company. 1964), v.

3. Frederick Taylor, *Scientific Management* (New York, NY: Harper and Row, Publishers, 1947).

4. Elton Mayo, *The Social Problems of an Industrial Civilization* (Boston, MA: Harvard Business School Press, 1945).

5. Lee Bolman and Terrence Deal, *Reframing Organizations* (San Francisco, CA: Jossey-Bass Publishers, 2003).

6. Fred Fiedler, *A Theory of Leadership Effectiveness* (New York, NY: McGraw-Hill Book Company, 1967).

7. Paul Hersey, *The Situational Leader* (New York, NY: Warner Books, Inc., 1984).

8. William Reddin, *Managerial Effectiveness* (New York, NY: Mc-Graw Hill Book Company, 1970).

9. Isabel Briggs Myers, *Gifts Differing* (Palo Alto, CA: Consulting Psychologists Press, Inc. 1980).

10. Rensis Likert, *The Human Organization* (New York, NY: McGraw-Hill Book Company, 1967).

11. Bernard Bass, *Bass and Stogdill's Handbook of Leadership* (New York, NY: The Free Press, 1990).

12. Lin Bothwell, *The Art of Leadership* (New York, NY: Prentice Hall Press, 1983).

13. Peter Drucker, *The Effective Executive* (New York, NY: Harper and Row Publishers, 1967), 22.

14. Jim Collins, *Good to Great* (New York, NY: Harper Business, 2001).

15. Joseph Badaracco Jr., *Leading Quietly* (Boston, MA: Harvard Business School Press, 2002), 1.

16. Eugene Jennings, *An Anatomy of Leadership: Princes, Heroes, and Supermen* (New York, NY: McGraw-Hill Book Company, 1960), xv.

17. Robert Sternberg, *The Triarchic Mind: A New Theory of Human Intelligence* (New York, NY: Viking Press, 1988).

18. Howard Gardner. *Frames of Mind: The Theory of Multiple Intelligences* (New York, NY: Basic Books, 1983).

19. Daniel Golman, *Emotional Intelligence* (New York, NY: Bantam Books, 1995).

20. Ralph Waldo Emerson, "An Address," in *The Complete Writings of Ralph Waldo Emerson*, Vol. I (New York, NY: Morrow, 1929).

21. Max Depree, *Leadership is an Art* (New York, NY: Doubleday, 1989).

22. Robert Bellah and others, *Habits of the Heart* (Berkeley, CA: University of California Press, 1985).

# CHAPTER

# Pressure and Profanity from the General Manager: Reflections on Leadership Effectiveness

*He has not learned the lesson of life who does not every day surmount a fear.*
—Ralph Waldo Emerson, *Essay on Courage*

*On the flip side of the ethics effectiveness continuum are situations where it is difficult to tell whether a leader is unethical, incompetent, or stupid.*
—Joanne Ciulla, *Ethics and Leadership Effectiveness*

My memory is that I was in a reasonably good mood as I left the house and drove to my office on a pleasant early summer morning some four years after accepting appointment as chancellor of Louisiana State University in Shreveport. Most of the staff knew that if I was whistling some happy tune that I was likely to be in a happy mood and so I was, walking down the hall and stopping to chat with the office staff and supervisor Sue Carroll.

While I was working over some administrivia on the desk, Sue put through a call from the general manager of one of the city's largest manufacturing plants. The call transformed my mood from a pleasant euphoria to full red alert in short order.

"Grady," the general manager opened in friendly and personal tone, "as you may know, our daughter enrolled at Vanderbilt last fall. It appears, however, that there may have been more fun and frolic than study and learning associated with her venture to the Music City. Vanderbilt placed her on academic suspension at the end of the spring term and so she's home underfoot. What's the possibility that we might be able to get her enrolled at LSUS?"

"Well, Bill," I replied, "what was her grade point average at the end of the year?"

"Well, ah, Grady, it's embarrassing to talk about. I believe that she had a 0.6 average on a 4.0 scale."

Bill was someone I had to look in the eye every Tuesday at downtown Rotary and was a well respected civic and corporate leader. And so I moved carefully into the conversation.

"Bill," I said, "we require a 1.8 GPA for transfer after taking that many hours during the first year, and your daughter falls well away from that standard."

"Well I had that pretty well figured out before I called you," he responded in a slightly more tense voice. "So here's what I want to know. Aren't you the chief executive of the university and aren't you empowered to make exceptions to policy?"

"The answer to both of your questions is yes," I responded.

"Okay. Are you going to make a policy exception for my daughter or not?" he queried.

"Before I answer your question, Bill, let me see if I understand what you're asking me to do. Is your position that you want Vanderbilt and other universities to adhere to their academic standards, but you don't want your state university here in Shreveport to honor its standards?" was the question I posed to Bill.

"Doesn't sound very good when you put it that way," he quipped.

"Let me ask the question another way," I continued. "Is your position that you want Vanderbilt and other universities to maintain their academic standards, but you are asking that your public state university become an academic half way house?"

Following some quick and sharply framed invective he hung up. End of story? No! Two days later, Bill called back and offered an apology. "Grady," he said, "you know that I was calling as a father the other day, but I had no business putting you on the spot like that and letting my language get sloppy. No, I don't want LSUS to dishonor its academic policies; and no, I don't want the university to serve as an academic dumping ground or half way house. What we're going to do is to let our daughter take the consequences of her own ill-considered decisions. You stand to duty and call me if you need me."

This opening narrative repeats a tactical leadership practice accented throughout these chapters and one to which I will return at the conclusion of this chapter—that the ability to frame a good question is an essential and highly useful leadership skill. There are several other lessons that may be gleaned from the experience.

## BEGRUDGING RESPECT AS AN EFFECTIVENESS INDICATOR

Folks assuming any leadership role do so with at least two theories in mind, a theory of role (what am I supposed to do) and a theory of effectiveness (how will I assess my success). Now these theories may reside at full awareness or subliminal levels, but they guide action at either level.

When one enters a dialogue about leadership effectiveness, the inevitable question turns on how we define the term. Every leader eventually operationally defines the term. Writing in his 1938 classic work *The Functions of the Executive*, Chester Barnard suggested that effectiveness is to be found in the accomplishment of recognized goals and objectives.[1] In his 1990 book *On Leadership*, John Gardner qualified this results approach to effectiveness, noting that financial and political conditions might weigh heavily on the achievement of goals.[2]

In the 1960's, most college presidents might have been counted "successful" or effective because conditions of both enrollment and financial growth made it almost certain that no matter the administrative behavior, colleges would get bigger and be financed with increasing support. Not so, however, for those presidents laboring in some states during the 1990s and moving into the early part of the 21st century.

A range of personal attributes has been aligned with leadership effectiveness. In their 1988 work *The Effective College President*, James Fisher, Martha Tack, and Kenneth Wheeler[3] described effective college presidents as self confident and positive, deeply committed to mission, confident in colleagues. In his 1979 work *The Effective Administrator*, Donald Walker suggested that *ineffective* collegiate leaders are occupied with status and position, regard critics as troublemakers, and are occupied with laziness and inertia.[4]

A variety of methods are employed to assess leadership effectiveness. Some institutions use a system of Management by Objectives, initially popularized in corporate leadership, in which achievement is measured against predetermined goals. Some use surveys containing evaluative items and Likert scales. Still others use consultant interview systems. The merits and forms of presidential evaluation have been engaged in a number of seminal publications in recent years.

In 1999, William Davis and Douglas Davis explored the merits of formal and informal evaluation of the college president and the question of what stakeholders (board members and faculty, for example) should have prime voice in such evaluations.[5] The Association of Governing Boards of Universities and Colleges published a manual on presidential assessment in June 1984, authored by John Nason,[6] and a national survey was sponsored and published by AGB in 1998, authored by Michael Schwartz.[7] Whatever the assessment method or instrument, all such evaluation mechanisms will constitute operational expressions and definitions of effectiveness.

Among the indicators that have been used as signals of effectiveness are these:

(1) Goal achievement
(2) Longevity in office
(3) Colleague growth and development
(4) Visibility and engagement in civic and professional affairs
(5) Constituent and stakeholder satisfaction
(6) Institutional performance (as depicted in performance indicators/report cards)

Readers interested in exploring the issue of performance indicators may find a 2001 journal piece by Steve Michael, Michael Schwartz, and Leela Bairaj of interest.[8] An important additional indicator from this article turns on presidential ability to attract resources.

What about the question of whether an effective leader is also an "ethical" leader, someone who is an ethical exemplar? Leadership Scholar Joanne Ciulla[9] offers a thoughtful and informing analysis on this question. She suggests that effectiveness has both a moral and technical dimension, as does John Gardner already cited. A leader may be ethical but ineffective in achieving goals, and a leader may be immoral but effective in achieving goals. We might add that a leader may be entirely effective in achieving unworthy or destructive goals.

Ciulla also highlights the issues of "moral luck" and "moral intent." In the former, an ethical leader may be caught in an unlucky moment. In the latter, the ethics of a particular action will turn on analysis of leader intent, methods employed, and results achieved. For additional and provoking dialogue on the sticky wicket of means and ends, see Saul Alinsky's *Rules for Radicals*[10] cited elsewhere in these reflections.

The evaluation of leadership balance sheets certainly belongs in the hands of those we serve. However, as we suggested in our opening chapter, there are many stakeholders who can make claim to a legitimate voice in the governance of our colleges and in the evaluation of administrative performance. For the president, these stakeholders will surely include members of the governing board as premier voices. Faculty, staff, students have an important voice because they are the ones who experience the inner effect of leadership style and values. Civic and political leaders bring external perspective. Some differences in perspective on the relative importance of faculty involvement may be found in the previously cited article by Davis and Davis, and articles by James Fisher and Gary Quehl[11] and by Kelly McKerrow and Lawrence Dennis.[12]

None of the previously listed performance indicators is without some technical or philosophical imperfection. Goal achievement is subject, as we've already noted, to financial and political climate. A genial office holder may manage to stay in office over a period of years with little achievement to show for the stay. Colleague initiative and investment may have as much to do with their growth as executive encouragement. Leader engagement in civic and professional affairs may be arranged as much for show and symbolism as for real caring. Popularity may be shallow and fleeting, less to be valued than a long term expression of trust and begrudging respect from constituents.

Martin Gilbert's 1991 biography of Winston Churchill details the defeat of the Conservative party in the summer of 1945 and Churchill's consequent loss of the Prime Minister's position immediately following his extraordinary and inspiring leadership of Britain during World War II.[13] This has to be one of the most surprising leadership moments in history and surely must have left Churchill reflecting on the question of leadership effectiveness. That Churchill emerged from this moment of defeat to once again become Prime Minister and to pen a significant history of World War II in his mature years is an equally impressive chronicle.

While there would hardly be a collegiate leader who would not yearn for the affirmation of his or her constituents, there are moments when we can be grateful if we have garnered the long term begrudging respect of our constituents, especially if we have honored a standard of excellence and integrity. This takes us to our second lesson.

## MORAL OUTRAGE AND OTHER SERVANTS OF QUALITY AND INTEGRITY

The January/February 1997 issue of *Trusteeship* carried a paper I authored and entitled "Moral Outrage and Other Servants of Quality." In that paper I remarked that American higher education has fashioned a diverse set of technical systems for defining, developing, and demonstrating quality. There are peer evaluation systems of accreditation, program review, and rankings/ratings. The assessment movement caused us to accent results/outcomes as much as process, accenting the concept of multiple evidences. Emphasizing customer satisfaction and continuous improvements, systems of Total Quality Management (TQM) were translated from corporate life into collegiate life. And some states mandated performance indicator reporting and performance budgeting/funding as instruments of quality assurance and accountability.

I noted in that article that "Quality assurance in our colleges and universities, however, is more than systems and technique, more than ciphers and computers. A faculty member with a caring touch and high standards may be more directly potent in the cause of quality than a good ranking in *U.S. News and World Report*, a well oiled TQM system, or a positive report of performance indicators. An academic administrator with courage, compassion, and integrity may more directly affect quality than any system of quality assurance."[14]

The importance of caring for standard, as illustrated in the opening narrative to this chapter, I learned in part from watching leadership mentors and models in my life. Dr. John Richardson was the long term Dean of Graduate Studies at the University of Memphis and was one of those responsible for opening opportunity for my career in college administration.

One day while I was visiting in his office, the dean took a call from a state senator apparently intent on getting a marginally qualified student into graduate school. Presuming that a touch of political pressure might ease the dean into an affirming response, the senator threatened a bit of political leverage. I watched as Dean Richardson's visage assumed a grim and determined fix, and his bulldog jowls began to shake as he spoke to the senator as follows: "Son, are you threatening me? Because if you are, I will come up to Big Sandy when next you run for office and campaign against you. And, son, I will defeat you." The dean's regard and stature in rural West Tennessee were such that he could have easily made good on his promise.

The probability that an accrediting team, a TQM report, an assessment exercise, or accountability report to the state legislature would have helped much on this point of quality and integrity is not high. This was about leadership caring and courage, about a collegiate leader who knew what was right and was willing to act. This was about leadership effectiveness. Lessons on caring and courage are, as Anne Colby and William Damon write in their 1992 book *Some Do Care*, more likely to be caught than taught.[15] In an extensive study dedicated to the question of what made some leaders hold to their integrity while under moral stress, they found their subjects talking less about their behavior as being courageous and more about dedication to a point of conviction. I think it fair to say that I "caught" this lesson in courage from Dr. John Richardson and others in my life, and I also was "taught" by the research described in Colby and Damon's thoughtful qualitative journey. *Some Do Care* ... our colleges and universities would be well served if more college leaders would just remember the title of their book and act on that memory.

## LEADING IN THE INTERROGATORY

As reflected in opening notes of this chapter and in other chapters, in my years as an educator, I have been struck with how important carefully crafted questions are to effective leadership and to effective teaching. Questions can be gentle instruments of discovery and discernment, of correction and encouragement. They may also be instruments of accusation and entrapment. They may be used to stimulate curiosity and to challenge arrogance. They may be deployed in calling others to responsibility, as emphasized in Chapter 2.

There is a natural urge for immediate response when we are asked a question, as was I when put on the spot by the general manager. Once someone has posed a question, we are placed on the defensive. However, we can return to the offense by posing a question in return. Leaders in all organizations are often inclined to the declarative and imperative in style, telling rather than asking. We can seriously enrich our style and our effectiveness, however, if we are willing to live a little more often in the interrogatory.

More years ago than I like to remember I played first chair French horn in our rural small town band in Millington, Tennessee. One afternoon close to the end of the rehearsal, we had just finished playing a march that ended *without* the traditional "stinger" note at the end. Thinking less of the music and more of the touch-football game that Larry, Walter, Herb and I would play after school, I let loose with a resounding stinger note, whose singular presence resounded around the band room rafters in lonely and loud traverse. My face turned crimson and I silently lamented the excellent acoustics of the hall, which allowed the note to bounce around for what seemed like an eternity. The band director leaned over the podium, with a smile on his face, and asked, "Grady, how did you know what note to play on that musical rest?"

In Chapter 2, I reported a dialogue with my new vice chancellor for Academic Affairs, one in which I was able to shape our dialogue on personnel evaluation with a couple of questions. In the opening of this chapter, I resisted the impulse for an immediate response to the general manager's question concerning whether I would make an exception to academic policy for his daughter. I chose, instead, to query his sense of values and responsibility. The theory of leadership role at work in that exchange was one of calling folks, whether colleagues or civic friends, to responsibility.

## THE INDEPENDENCE OF SOLITUDE

Two lines from Emerson's essay on "Self Reliance" spring to memory here. The first of these is: "Nothing is at last sacred but the integrity of your own mind. . . . Trust thyself, every heart vibrates to that iron string."[16] And the second is as follows: "The great man is he who in the midst of the crowd keeps with perfect sweetness the independence of solitude."[17] The friendship of one's own conscience is also not an infallible indicator of effectiveness, but it is a useful anchor.

Let me close these reflections on leadership effectiveness with this narrative. In the late 1980s, Louisiana Governor Buddy Roemer commissioned a statewide blue ribbon task force to explore ways to desegregate the Louisiana System of Higher Education more effectively. It has always been my conviction that the governor's hidden agenda in this venture was to explore possible changes in the governance structure of colleges and universities in the state.

Close to the end of one task force meeting in Baton Rouge, Chairman Joe Smith asked me as chancellor of LSU Shreveport and Dr. Dan Reneau, president of Louisiana Tech University, to bring a report to the next meeting of the Task Force, a report that might explore possible merger of our two schools. Chairman Smith then summarily adjourned the meeting.

I was furious and drove in a dark funk the 200 miles back to Shreveport. I stopped by the office and framed a letter to Mr. Smith, which I placed in FED-EX delivery. More on the content of the letter in a moment.

When I arrived home, my wife Linda handed me pink phone slips from newspaper reporters in Shreveport and Baton Rouge. I called the reporter with the Shreveport Times who opened by saying, "Chancellor Bogue, we've learned that you have been directed by the chair of the Governor's blue ribbon task force to draw a merger plan with Louisiana Tech. Will you be drawing that plan, Sir?"

"No, I will not," I replied.

"Sir, are you going to defy the chair of the governor's task force?" she countered.

"Well, let's think about this together. This blue ribbon task force was charged with exploring ways to desegregate higher education more effectively in the state. If I were to work on a merger plan, I would be the first college president in the nation to attempt an improvement in desegregation by merging two predominantly white institutions! Think of it. My campus is sixty miles from Louisiana Tech; and Grambling University, a historically black campus, is just two miles from Louisiana Tech. This request or directive is not about desegregation. It's about big time athletics. Louisiana Tech aspires to build its intercollegiate athletic program to NCAA Division I status and the population base of Shreveport would help Tech realize that goal."

I continued, "Now as to whether I am defying anyone, let me say this. The last time I looked, I reported to the president of the LSU system, Dr. Alan Copping, and through him to the LSU Board of Supervisors. At such time as I am directed by the LSU president and board to draw a merger plan I will do so or resign as chancellor if I think that a bad idea."

The next morning's issue of the *Shreveport Times* carried my picture on one side of the front page and President Reneau's picture on the other, with Dan saying that if I did not intend to work on a merger plan, he could hardly do so by himself. The content of my remarks to the reporter constituted the heart of my earlier cited FEDEX letter to Chairman Joe Smith. The matter of the merger was never discussed in future meetings of the task force.

This relationship with Joe Smith has a happy ending, so here's "the rest of the story." Joe was a well respected civic leader in Louisiana, the editor of the major paper in Alexandria and former chair of the Louisiana Board of Regents, the state's regulatory coordinating board. My dissent with Joe on this point notwithstanding, I had high regard for his civic leadership. A few months after the events reported here, Joe was appointed to the LSU Board of Supervisors and became one of my bosses so to speak.

In February 1990, after having served LSU Shreveport for almost ten years, I tendered my resignation as chancellor and gave the University a year to find a replacement, my resignation being effective for December 31, 1990. I felt that I needed renewal and that the university needed fresh energy and perspective. Another factor that played into this decision was that my three young children, all having been born while I served in Shreveport, were approaching their teen years, and I wanted to be able to spend time with them during those formative years.

When my wife Linda and I were about to enter my final board meeting in New Orleans in December of 1990, Joe Smith came up to me outside the meeting and said, "Grady, if it's okay with you I would like to have the pleasure of placing a motion on the Board agenda naming you chancellor emeritus, and I want you to know why. Over the years, you and I've had a number of interactions, when I served as chair of the Board of Regents and when I served as chair of the Governor's Task Force. We agreed on some things and disagreed on a few things. But I always considered you a man of honor and felt that you would speak the truth no matter what the issue was. And it's for that reason that I would like to have this point of personal privilege today."

There were a number of emotions pent up inside as I said, "Joe, I can't think of anyone from whom I would be more appreciative to see such a motion presented. I would be honored." And so with Joe's initiative and the LSU Board of Supervisor's approval, I received honorable discharge and have that framed formal resolution designating me as chancellor emeritus hanging on my study wall today.

Beyond the more obvious indicators of leadership performance cited in this reflection and elsewhere in the literature, the friendship of one's own conscience and the long term respect of those with whom you have served would be important indicators of leadership effectiveness in my value system. Consider this closing note. What's an essential inclination and skill for the collegiate leader who wants to be effective? That's a good question! A double entendre makes a nice ending here.

## NOTES

1. Chester Barnard, *The Functions of the Executive* (Cambridge, MA: The Harvard University Press, 1938).

2. John Gardner, *On Leadership* (New York, NY: The Free Press, 1990).

3. James Fisher, Martha Tack, and Kenneth Wheeler, *The Effective College President* (New York, NY: American Council on Education/MacMillan, 1988).

4. Donald Walker, *The Effective Administrator* (San Francisco, CA: Jossey-Bass Publishers, 1979).

5. William Davis and Douglas Davis, "The University Presidency: Do Evaluations Make a Difference," *Journal of Personnel Evaluation in Education* 2 (1999): 119–40.

6. John Nason, *Presidential Assessment: A Guide to the Periodic Review of the Performance of Chief Executives* (Washington, DC: Association of Governing Boards of Universities and Colleges, 1984).

7. Michael Schwartz, *A National Survey of Presidential Performance Assessment Policies and practices: AGB Occasional Paper No. 34* (Washington, DC: Association of Governing Boards of Universities and Colleges, 1998).

8. Steve Michael, Michael Schwartz, and Leela Bairaj, "Indicators of Presidential Effectiveness: A Study of Trustees of Higher Education Institutions," *The International Journal of Educational Management* 15, no. 7 (2001): 332–46.

9. Joanne Ciulla, "Ethics and Leadership Effectiveness," in *The Nature of Leadership*, ed. Antonakis, J., Cianciolo, A., and Sternberg, R. (Thousand Oaks, CA: Sage Publications, 2004).

10. Saul Alinsky, *Rules for Radicals* (New York, NY: Random House, Inc., 1971).

11. James Fisher, and Gary Quehl, "Presidential Assessment: Obstacles to Leadership," *Change* 4 (1984): 5–7.

12. Kelly McKerrow, and Lawrence Dennis, "Evaluation of University Presidents: Broadening the Perspective," *The Journal of Education Thought* 1 (1989): 3–14.

13. Martin Gilbert, *Churchill: A New Life* (New York, NY: Holt, 1991).

14. E. Grady Bogue, "Moral Outrage and Other Servants of Quality," *Trusteeship* 1 (1997): 11.

15. Anne Colby, and William Damon, *Some do care* (New York, NY: The Free Press, 1992).

16. Ralph Waldo Emerson, "Self reliance," in *The Complete Writings of Ralph Waldo Emerson*, Vol. 1 (New York, NY: Morrow, 1929), 138–39.

17. Ibid., 140.

# CHAPTER 12

## Questions of Accountability: Linking Cultures of Evidence and Cultures of Faith

*In measuring things that can be counted or expressed in quantifiable terms, we are led unawares to the grand illusion—that only the measurable really matters.*
—Harold Enarson, "University or Knowledge Factory," *Chronicle of Higher Education*, June 18, 1973.

Those holding leadership responsibility in any organization are responsible for both individual and institutional effectiveness, for their own performance and the performance of the unit or organization which they hold in trust. We have spoken of the former. Let us speak of the latter, the question of whether our campuses are performing effectively.

In the fall of 1974, I took leave from my appointment as assistant vice president for Academic Affairs at the University of Memphis and went to work for a year with the Tennessee Higher Education Commission (THEC), a state level coordinating agency for public colleges and universities in the state. The one year appointment at THEC was associated with my selection as an American Council on Education Fellow in Academic Administration for the class of 1974–75. I had asked for the fellowship year to be taken with THEC so that I could work with Dr. John Folger, the executive director, as mentor.

My interest in working with Dr. Folger turned on a policy question that we had framed concerning the allocation of state funds to institutions in the state. That question was as follows: Was it feasible to allocate some portion of state funds on a performance criterion rather than an enrollment or activity criterion? Dr. Folger had been watching the political accountability and assessment expectations being imposed upon elementary and secondary education and thought a pro-active initiative on the part of higher education would be wise.

I thought this was a provocative policy challenge. Before departing the University of Memphis, I was advised by friends and colleagues there and over the state that I would find the answer to the question would be "No," from both technical and philosophical perspectives, and that I probably should find other engagement for my fellowship year.

I thought otherwise. During my ACE Fellowship year, we secured $500,000 in grant support to launch a partnership inquiry involving campus, board, and state government (executive and legislative) representatives and a national advisory panel.

The five-year, developmental policy journey on this performance and accountability question is reported in the final 1980 project report by E. Grady Bogue and William Troutt,[1] in E. Grady Bogue and Wayne Brown's 1982 paper appearing in the *Harvard Business Review*,[2] and in a 2002 book chapter by E. Grady Bogue[3] appearing in a Rockefeller Institute Press book written by Joseph Burke and Associates. Performance Funding policy in Tennessee allocates a portion of state funds (5.45 percent) to campuses based on five performance criteria, and the policy is now in its twenty-fifth year of operation.

There were many memorable moments in that five-year journey of planning and implementation. Three I remember in particular. Dr. William Troutt, now president of Rhodes College and for many years president of Belmont University, was Assistant Director and colleague on this policy project. I can remember many days on which Bill and I rode around in his vintage brown Ford Mustang, wondering if either of us had chosen a wise career path in venturing into this policy and political thicket.

In retrospect, the journey did not seem to disadvantage either one of us. I invested eleven years as college president in the public sector at LSU Shreveport and my brief interim at LSU Baton Rouge (and Agricultural and Mechanical College!) and Bill has invested close to a quarter century as president of two splendid private colleges, Belmont University and Rhodes College. Both of our dads wore overalls and plowed behind mules in the dirt of rural West Tennessee, an honorable work. That Bill and I had opportunity to plow a new kind of ground in the performance funding project is tribute to the opportunities provided us in American public and private higher education.

The second memory flows from a conference Bill and I held with campus presidents in Nashville. In that meeting, we explored program and institutional accreditation as a performance indicator. Some of the presidents were critical of using accreditation, suggesting that it was not really a credible measure of campus quality and performance. "If this is the case, then," I suggested to those assembled, "let's take all references to institutional and program accreditation out of our catalogs, view books, and other public relations documents."

"Well, wait a moment. That's not what we had in mind," replied the presidents.

"Can we have it both ways?" I queried. "Can we trumpet accreditation in our publications as a quality indicator and reject accreditation as a quality and performance indicator for consideration in this policy?"

Accreditation became one of the five original performance indicators. At the time of policy implementation in 1980, only two-thirds of programs over the state that were eligible for accreditation were actually accredited. Within a decade, that percentage topped out at 100 percent.

In a visit with academic deans at the University of Tennessee-Knoxville during the late 1970s planning years, we explored whether another performance indicator related to general education might be developed. At this time in the late 1970s, only a couple of institutions in the state were doing any assessment of general education outcomes. Bill and I queried the UT Deans on whether there was any common intellectual expectation for their various bachelor's degrees. The answer was "No." I then turned to the UTK catalog and pointed to the degree requirement page that described a 12-hour English requirement for all bachelor's degrees at the University and asked what that meant. With a little reluctant backtracking, the deans admitted that perhaps this did represent a common intellectual expectation.

In the final version of the performance funding policy crafted by the committee of campus, board, and political representatives, a general education outcome indicator was required, but no particular assessment of outcome test was required in the policy, leaving the choice of assessment methodology and instrumentation to each campus. As it turned out, in the first iteration of the policy, all twenty-one campuses in the state elected to use the recently developed American College Testing Program College Outcome Measures Performance (COMP) instrument.

## EMERGENCE OF ACCOUNTABILITY POLICY

The Tennessee performance funding policy was a venture in quality assurance and accountability. In the latter half of the 20th century, accountability became an ascendant policy accent for American higher education. That policy accent continues in this first decade of the 21st century. To what extent, however, do higher education's many stakeholders and academic leaders hold common perspectives on the definition and purpose, the evidence and the effectiveness of accountability policy and practice? In this reflection, we intend to probe the questions that accountability poses for higher education performance, and we intend to probe questions about the meaning of accountability and the effectiveness of accountability policy.

The "accountability" policy movement picked up momentum primarily in the last third of the 20th century. Regional accrediting agencies and some professional accrediting associations moved from process indicators to educational outcomes and institutional effectiveness indicators. Testing students for what they know, the emergence of the assessment movement, was yet another expression of increased accountability expectations. State governments became a more assertive external player in public higher education accountability policy, issuing regulations and laws that mandated assessment practices and called for performance indicator reports.

Another accountability policy expression, performance funding and budgeting systems, represented a mix of internal and external policy initiatives. Tennessee's venture into performance funding policy we described in our opening remarks. That state's policy links annual performance indicators to campus funding. The policy has been operative now for a quarter century. In a contrasting policy venture, the state of South Carolina experienced a legislatively imposed policy that proved unworkable over a few short years, and the policy was eventually abandoned.

Individual campuses, multi campus systems, and national policy agencies added to the accountability impulse in the United States with "Report Card" policies. Numerous boards and their campuses have adopted such report cards. On the use of report cards as an instrument of higher education accountability, probably no accountability policy initiative has provoked as much discussion and debate as the 2000 publication of the National Center for Public Policy and Higher Education's *Measuring Up 2000* (reissued in 2002, 2004, and 2006).[4] Here we have an independently funded, non-governmental policy agency undertaking a performance assessment of entire state systems and publishing the comparative results on six criteria: preparation, participation, affordability, completion, benefits, and learning.

Two reports, one from 1972 and one from 2005, furnish conceptual bookends to the political and professional dialogue on higher education accountability over a third of a century. Kenneth Mortimer's 1972 monograph entitled *Accountability in Higher Education* was an early and high visible entry.[5] Mortimer delineated multiple stakeholders in his discussion of external (courts, legislatures, accrediting agencies, etc.) and internal accountability interests (faculty, students, boards of trustees) and suggested that accountability centers on educational results, on outcomes rather than inputs.

Noting this emphasis on "educational results" by Mortimer, we jump thirty years to a 2005 report released by the National Commission on Accountability in Higher Education. *Accountability for Better Results: A National Imperative for Higher Education* also places emphasis on "results" and features accountability as an "imperative."[6] The 2005 report was the outcome of a special study commission created by the State Higher Education Executive Officers (SHEEO), a national organization of coordinating board executive officers. Here we find the policy voice of a national governance group of higher educational administrators, government officials, and corporate officers.

In the interim, in 1996, Graham, Lyman, and Trow authored a policy report entitled *Accountability in Colleges and Universities* that was also an important contribution to the accountability dialogue.[7] In this report, the authors explored what they called the paradox of public esteem, noting that Americans continue to place high value on higher education even as pressures for accountability escalate.

More recently, in 2006, the Secretary of Education's Commission on the Future of Higher Education has spiced up the dialogue with discussion of a national assessment option and issuance of policy papers on accreditation and accountability-assessment. Two of these concept papers include Robert Dickenson's "The Need for Accreditation Reform"[8] and Charles Miller and Geri Malandra's paper "Accountability/Assessment."[9] Debate over the Commission's proposals and issue papers was featured in subsequent articles appearing in the *Chronicle of Higher Education*, an article by Kelly Field[10] in the April 7, 2006, issue and another by Bruce Bollag[11] in the April 14, 2006, issue.

A brief diversion may prove informing as we consider the more general case of public sector governance and management. Writing in the March 2005 issue of *Public Performance and Management Review*, Melvin Dubnick suggested that accountability challenges traditional governance models that had the bureaucratic liabilities of being self seeking, turf protecting, and dehumanizing and that offered ponderous structures unresponsive and indifferent to the clients they were intended to serve.[12] He further advanced the idea that accountability serves to promote "transparency" in governmental operations, to place performance on top of the dialogue table and in the limelight of public scrutiny. More importantly, however, Dubnick challenged the widely held assumption that greater accountability will improve public management and performance.

In illustration, Dubnick cites the case of the United States 1993 Government Performance and Report Act which required all federal agencies to prepare five year strategic plans linked to measurable outcomes, and to use these outcomes as the foundation of annual performance reports. It would appear, according to Dubnick, that this governmental accountability policy turned into a ponderous and largely symbolic exercise—an exercise failing to deliver on the performance improvements expected.

The dialogue on accountability is taking place against the backdrop of what Katherine Lyall and Kathleen Sell describe as the de facto privatization of public higher education–reduction in state appropriations in recent years, rapid and continuous rise in student tuition, higher education seen as private benefit rather than a public benefit, political pressures to reduce size and involvement of government, application of market principles in higher education management, and the moves in some states to privatize entire institutions or major programs/professional schools within institutions.[13] We earlier touched on this pressure to privatize in Chapter 1.

While meritorious, the intent of accountability policy to encourage attention to performance questions may not be matched by desired outcomes, in government or in the more specific case of higher education. In higher education, for example, campus response to some accountability policy may be cosmetic and adaptive . . . and in some cases downright dishonest. The misinformation on data submitted by some U.S. institutions to the *U.S. News and World Report* publication *America's Best Colleges* may be taken in partial example. If an MBA program is to be ranked on the basis of GMAT scores, one option of influencing a more positive ranking is to admit students with lower scores into their first year of study in a Master of Science program and then move these students to the MBA the second year. The merit and liabilities of these rankings and the deceits practiced in response to them constitute an interesting accountability narrative.

Finally, there may be contradictions in accountability expectations. Following the rules may conflict with professional judgment. In one state, an isolated instance of government automobile abuse caused the state finance officer to require pre-travel approval all the way to the state level for the use of state cars. A campus president could send a plane load of people across country with only campus approval but could not authorize the travel of one person out of state via automobile without the cumbersome approval process.

## DEFINITIONS, ASSUMPTIONS, AND QUESTIONS

As previously noted, American higher education lives with public salute and public scrutiny—simultaneously praised and maligned, acclaimed and criticized. This paradox, however, should not prove too surprising, given the tensioned mission expectations Americans have for their colleges as presented in Chapter 1.

What exactly does the term accountability mean and what are the major assumptions underwriting the concept? In our 2003 book *Quality and Accountability in Higher Education*, Kimberely Hall and I define accountability as a formal policy that:

(1) requires evaluation of both administrative and educational services,
(2) asks for public evidence of program and service performance,
(3) encourages independent/external review of such performance evidence, and
(4) requests information on the relationship between dollars spent and results achieved.[14]

A crisp definition of the term is found in Barbara Romzek's 2000 paper entitled "Dynamics of Public Sector Accountability in an Era of Reform" and appearing in the *International Review of Administrative Sciences*.[15] She defines accountability as "answerability for performance."

These definitions and previous commentary point to essential expectations of accountability policy. First is the expectation that accountability invites evidence on the effective, efficient, and honest use of resources. Second is the expectation that accountability invites evidence on learning outcomes—demonstrating changes in student knowledge, skill, and value while also demonstrating student ability to do work honorable and efficient and participating meaningfully in a democratic society. Third, is the expectation that accountability invites evidence on the extent to which goals and mission are being achieved—whether at program, campus, system, or state level. Perhaps not quite as obvious, but nonetheless important, is the expectation that integrity will be exemplified in the work and behavior of those faculty and administrators to whom colleges are entrusted for stewardship.

What assumptions accompany these expectations of accountability policy? One is that effective accountability policy will improve educational practice and outcomes. The second is that effective accountability policy will improve management and stewardship of resources. For some educational stakeholders, a third assumption is that effective accountability policy will improve financial and civic support for higher education.

These expectations and assumptions suggest a set of questions that mark the complexity of the concept and show why policy dialogue often assumes a facile and surface understanding that overlooks a serious complexity in the concept of accountability.

## STAKEHOLDERS/PRINCIPALS

To whom is higher education accountable? There are obviously multiple stakeholders: internal stakeholders of students, faculty, administrators and external stakeholders of boards, legislators, civic, corporate leaders. Do these stakeholders define their expectation of accountability purpose in the same way (to prove or to improve) and to what extent are the expectations of accountability a function of stakeholder role/interests?

### Mission

How will policy implementation and the kinds of evidence required support institutional mission complexity and diversity? Diversity has long been considered a major strength of American higher education. Will accountability policy recognize mission diversity and heritage or offer subtle pressures for mission conformity?

### Purpose

Will accountability policy highlight the economic development and workforce readiness purposes of higher education but neglect other educational purposes that include personal discovery and development, civic awareness and responsibility, and social justice and equity? Is the purpose of higher education to produce human capital or enhance human promise and potential? Or both? Is higher education a public or private good? Or both?

### Performance Evidence

What evidence will stakeholders accept as legitimate and adequate? Just as there is more complexity to the concept of accountability than may be revealed in casual dialogue, there is more complexity to the concept of performance than we pause to recognize. Will performance be measured in process (adherence to fiscal regulation and audit policy), in production (retention rates, number and percentage of bachelor's graduates), in competence (number and percentage of Ph.D faculty), in results (licensure pass rates and general education outcomes), or in productivity (cost per credit hour or degree completion)?

### Standard

Once the acceptable indicators or evidences of accountability have been framed there remains the question of evaluating the "goodness" of the performance. Will the standard be one of legal compliance, of good practice, of comparison to some criterion or peer reference?

## Communication

How can accountability evidence be clearly and concisely communicated so that stakeholders pay attention and believe the data? Is it possible to "be good" and not "look good"? The converse is that might we "look good" but not really "be good," that we have engaged in cosmetic and adaptive behaviors that furnish a performance patina, a shallow and surface record rather than a substantive performance record.

## Trust

Does it make a difference who gathers and presents the data on accountability? Will stakeholders accept data prepared and presented by those under accountability scrutiny, or will they insist on disinterested, third-party information acquisition as a condition of trust? Will audits eventually involve both financial and educational performance reviews? Might state governments adopt some form of "operational readiness inspection" as practiced in some military services, where review/evaluation teams descend unannounced on a campus to check its fiscal integrity and educational performance?

## Integrity

Will occasional acts of individual administrator and faculty wrongdoing or ethical misbehavior outweigh accountability reports? Is just one act of duplicity among faculty and administrators one too many for an institution expected to prepare leadership for every sector of our national life? Will educational/fiscal performance reports hold their value if newspapers are filled with accounts of faculty or administrator duplicity?

## STAKEHOLDER PERSPECTIVES:
## POINTS OF CONSENT AND DISSENT

A cluster of dissertation studies conducted in 2004–05 by Robertson-Scott,[16] Tanner,[17] and Tipton-Rogers[18] at the University of Tennessee explored the assumptions and perspectives of academic, corporate, and political leaders in the state on questions related to accountability purpose, method, and evidence. Before we explore the findings of these studies, here are important contextual notes.

Among higher education accountability policy instruments currently in place in Tennessee are (1) the Master Plan for Higher Education, with the most recent version approved in April 2005 by the Tennessee Higher Education Commission (THEC), (2) Formula Funding Policy for requesting and equitably allocating state appropriations to campuses (revised by THEC in 2005), (3) Performance Funding policy, which allocates 5.45 percent of state appropriations to campuses on a set of performance criteria and standards rather than enrollments (revised by THEC 2005), (4) State financial audit requirements, (5) Accreditation, and (6) Performance Indicator Reporting (*The Condition of Higher Education in Tennessee—2005*).

Earlier noted in Chapter 8, during the period of this study, four Tennessee public university presidents came under public scrutiny for ethical concerns. Two presidents of the University of Tennessee system departed within two years of one another, one for sexual misconduct and one for misuse of public funds. Presidents of two university campuses in the Board of Regents system came under review, one for charges of sexual harassment and the other for fiscal mismanagement.

## Commonality in Perception

Here are perceptions held in common by the three stakeholder groups of academic, legislative, and corporate leaders. There was:

- A united belief that higher education accountability is not a passing policy fad and that accountability will remain a policy accent for higher education in coming years.
- A clear notion that accountability means fiscal stewardship: the effective, the efficient, and the honest utilization of resources entrusted to colleges and universities.
- The expectation that campuses will offer evidence on student learning outcomes. There was less certainty on the specific form of such evidence and how higher education might satisfy the interest of multiple stakeholders on educational performance and simultaneously reflect diversity of mission.
- The expectation that higher education will be responsive to community and state needs, with this expectation most often cast in economic and workforce development terms.
- An awareness that higher education has multiple accountability stakeholders, with some consent on the idea that students are the ones to whom colleges owe first accountability debt.
- Consent that acts of administrative wrong doing negatively affect perceptions of management competence/integrity and overshadow written accountability reports.
- A conviction that presence of accountability policy is not necessarily a guarantor of enhanced financial support for or satisfaction with higher education, nor was there clear conviction that the quality and effectiveness of college management are improved.

## A Policy Challenge

What might be considered surprising and perhaps disappointing from these studies? As just noted, there was an absence of preciseness on accountability definition, acceptable evidence, and decision purpose among different stakeholder groups. There appeared to be an absence of trust, an absence of awareness, and an absence of partnership reflected in the perspectives of political and corporate leaders.

Legislative and corporate leaders expressed little awareness of the many policy instruments and data that academic officers might see as elements of policy accountability systems: master planning, formula funding, performance funding, indicator reporting, and fiscal audits. Is the public accountability expectation this simple: "Spend money wisely and honestly, send us graduates who can contribute to the workforce and economy, and hire academic leaders with integrity?"

Legislative and corporate officers mentioned with great frequency the mission of colleges and universities as instruments of economic development and workforce readiness but mentioned less frequently the mission of higher education as an instrument of personal discovery and development, as a guarantor of civic awareness and democracy's health, and as contributor to cultural enrichment.

A disappointing and troubling finding was that legislative leaders did not trust the data furnished by campus and governing board officers in both public testimony and in written reports . . . but did trust information supplied by the State Comptroller. This raises the question of whether there should be a system of both financial and educational performance audits conducted by a disinterested party, such as the State Comptroller/Auditor.

## THE CASE AND CALL FOR PARTNERSHIP

The call for stronger partnership in the design and implementation of higher education accountability policy systems was reflected in the comments of legislators and corporate leaders interviewed. The call of the partnership trumpet may be clarion in intent if less certain on method, on what evidence will prove acceptable, and on how to acquire and present that evidence.

When external stakeholders stand off in grand detachment to lob shells of critique at accountability reports, when there has been little or no initial consent on accountability policy purpose and evidence, we may rightly ask how effective policy will be, whether in proving stewardship or improving performance. It will surely be easier for criticism of higher education purpose and performance to emerge when there is limited awareness of or allegiance to the multiple missions of higher education. And it will be easier for criticism of higher education purpose and performance to emerge when cultures of fact and evidence (what we know) and cultures of faith (what we believe, hope and value) are not balanced.

"Acting on the Possible While Awaiting Perfection" was the motto adopted by the Tennessee higher education community thirty years ago when pilot projects and dialogue were opened on Tennessee Performance Funding Policy described in opening comments of this chapter. The dialogue continues and the policy continues, a policy continually reviewed and adapted in purpose and process. Linking civic and collegiate decision interests, linking cultures of evidence and cultures of faith may be advanced in these ways:

(1) A partnership dialogue on accountability policy purpose, evidence, and system as outlined in this discussion may be encouraged as a means of enhancing policy understanding and design.
(2) Civic friends may take some pleasure in that two long-standing evidences of accountability, accreditation (both institutional and program) and financial audits, remain respected instruments.
(3) Partnership forums may serve as two-way communication conduits—conveying to civic, political, and corporate friends an interpretation of the complex mission expectations of colleges and bringing to campus leaders the hopes and concerns of civic, political, and corporate leaders.
(4) Faculty and collegiate leaders should be exemplars in framing evidence related to goal achievement on their campuses.
(5) Faculty and collegiate leaders should take initiative in designing intelligence and/or indicator profiles that provide trend data and current data related to programs, personnel, finance, student abilities and achievement. And they may design these indicator profiles to furnish a crisp operational expression of what is central to the distinction and mission of the institution.

## DECISION, DISCOVERY, DISTINCTION

Collegiate leaders hold in trust a precious and complex enterprise. Asking questions of purpose and performance and creating cultures of evidence and accountability are as appropriate and essential for our colleges and universities as they are for any organization. Effective accountability policy is an instrument for improving decisions, for learning and making discovery about our institutions, and for making visible the heritage and distinction of a campus.

A beautiful line found in Kahlil Gibran's *Sand and Foam* notes that "Your mind and my heart will never agree until your mind ceases to live in the numbers and my heart in the mist."[19] Not all that is true, not all that is real, and not all that is beautiful lies in the numbers, in cultures of evidence. Colleges are communities of personal caring and civic faith, where student vision is lifted from the poverty of the commonplace. They are crucibles of dissent where yesterday's heresy becomes today's common sense. They are places where the compulsive curiosity of man is celebrated and encouraged. Collegiate leaders are guardians and custodians of such places, places where the call to accountability is one of majestic complexity . . . but not a call to be neglected.

## NOTES

1. E. Grady Bogue and William Troutt, *Allocation of State Funds on a Performance Criterion* (Nashville, TN: Tennessee Higher Education Commission, 1980).

2. E. Grady Bogue and Wayne Brown, "Performance Incentives for State Colleges," *Harvard Business Review* 60 (1982): 123–28.

3. E. Grady Bogue, "Twenty Years of Performance Funding in Tennessee: A Case Study of Policy Intent and Effectiveness," in *Funding Public Colleges for Performance*, ed. Joseph Burke and Associates (Albany, NY: Rockefeller Institute Press, 2002), 85–105.

4. Measuring Up: The National Report Card on Higher Education (Palo Alto, CA: National Policy Center for Higher Education, 2000, 2002, 2004, 2006).

5. Kenneth Mortimer, *Accountability in Higher Education* (Washington, DC: American Association for Higher Education, 1972).

6. *Accountability for Better Results: A National Imperative for Higher Education* National Commission on Accountability in Higher Education. (Denver, CO: State Higher Education Executive Officers, 2005).

7. Patricia Graham, Richard Lyman, and Martin Trow, *Accountability of Colleges and Universities* (New York, NY: Columbia University October, 1995).

8. Robert Dickenson, *Issue Paper: The Need for Accreditation Reform* (Washington, DC: The Secretary of Education's Commission on the Future of Higher Education, March 31, 2006).

9. Charles Miller and Geri Malandra, *Issue Paper: Accountability/Assessment* (Washington, DC: The Secretary of Education's Commission on the Future of Higher Education, March 31, 2006).

10. Kelly Field, "Panel to Give Colleges 'Gentle Shove' Toward Testing," *The Chronicle of Higher Education* 52 (April 7, 2006): A33.

11. Bruce Bollag, "Federal Panel Floats Plan to Overhaul Accreditation," *The Chronicle of Higher Education* 52 (April 14, 2006): A1.

12. Melvin Dubnick, "Accountability and the Promise of Performance: In Search of the Mechanisms. *Public Performance and Management Review* 28, no. 3 (March, 2005): 376–417.

13. Katherine Lyall and Kathleen Sell, *The True Genius of America at Risk: Are We Losing our Public Universities to De Facto Privatization?* (Westport, CT: ACE/Praeger, 2006).

14. E. Grady Bogue and Kimberely Bingham Hall, *Quality and Accountability in Higher Education* (Westport, CT: Praeger, 2003).

15. Barbara Romzek, "Dynamics of Public Sector Accountability in an Era of Reform," *International Review of Administrative Sciences* 66 (2000): 21–44.

16. Kristi Roberson-Scott, Tennessee Higher Education Accountability Policies and Practices: State Legislative Perspective. Unpublished doctoral dissertation (Knoxville, TN:University of Tennessee, 2005).

17. Sharon Tanner, The Effectiveness of Accountability Policy in Higher Education: The Perspective of Higher Education Leaders. Unpublished doctoral dissertation (Knoxville, TN: University of Tennessee, 2005).

18. Donna Tipton-Rogers, Higher Education Accountability: A Corporate Perspective. Unpublished doctoral dissertation (Knoxville, TN: University of Tennessee, 2004).

19. Kahlil Gibran, *Sand and Foam* (New York, NY: Alfred A. Knopf, 1973), 23.

# AFTERWORD

## A Friend of Mind: The Cultivation of a Sustaining Curiosity

*I fear the popular notion of success stands in direct opposition in all points to the real and wholesome success. One adores public opinion, the other private opinion: one fame, the other desert; one feats, the other humility; one lucre, the other love; one monopoly, and the other hospitality of mind.*

—Ralph Waldo Emerson, *Success*

*If the leader is just an expediter of what other people want, a 'resource' for their use, the people are not being led, but serviced.*

—Garry Wills, *Certain Trumpets*

Most books open with a Preface and/or Foreword. How many books end with an Afterword I do not know, but the term seemed appropriate for these closing reflections.

Twenty years after I received the first doctoral degree awarded by the University of Memphis, I was invited back to the campus as speaker for the May 7, 1988, commencement celebration. In the room where faculty and platform party were putting on their robes in preparation, I was subjected to much good natured kidding, including the observation that the quality of graduate students had been increasing since the day I received my doctoral degree.

This friendly jousting reminded me of a rejection notice sent by a Chinese economics journal to the author of a paper to this effect: "If we were to publish your paper, it would be impossible for us to publish any work of lower standard. And as it is unthinkable that in the next thousand years we shall see its equal, we are, to our regret, compelled to return your divine composition, and to beg you a thousand times to overlook our short sight and timidity."[1] The friendly comments of former colleagues notwithstanding, I would like to hope that there is little in my professional record to give the University any reason to be apologetic about having conferred that first doctorate on me.

As faculty and stage party lined up for departure to the coliseum floor, a faculty friend from my earlier ten years at the University whispered in my ear, "Grady, if you speak more than ten minutes, I will stand up in the middle of graduation and salute you with an obscene gesture, a gesture commonly known as 'the bird.'"

In a number of commencement addresses, I tried always to remember that commencement is a day for the students to celebrate and not a day for long-winded speeches. Thus, it was not so difficult to respond to my friend's good natured threat. When I stood to address the graduating students, I suggested that I could complete my remarks inside of five minutes. This brought an ovation before I had begun the address. My five-minute address entitled "A Friend of Mine" was later carried in *Vital Speeches of Today* and may have been one of the shortest and best set of public remarks I framed over my career.[2] I had intended and written the title as "A Friend of Mind," but apparently the editors of *Vital Speeches* decided that this was a spelling error and revised it.

Before offering summary reflections in closing these essays on collegiate leadership, I want to say first that I am filled with a profound sense of gratitude that I've enjoyed more than forty years as administrator and professor in an organization whose purposes are to advance truth and to advance the promise of human talent. I am filled as well with an appreciative sense of wonder and pleasure that our society will support with its resources and allegiance—and, yes, its critical scrutiny—an organization whose purposes also include the critical review/evaluation of policy and practice in every field of endeavor.

## WHAT I HAVE LEARNED

In 1966, Norman Cousins edited a book entitled *What I Have Learned*, wherein some dozen major public figures from writer Alan Paton to General Dwight Eisenhower framed essay reflections on what they had learned. There are words of wisdom to be found in every essay in Cousin's book but none more elevating than this line found in Alan Paton's essay on "The Challenge of Fear: " "Life has taught me—and this is my luck—that active loving saves one from a morbid preoccupation with the shortcomings of society and the waywardness of men."[3]

So, over the years what have I learned about leading in colleges and universities?

- Model the value of compassion, as leading and loving are fundamentally acts of caring.
- Mark arrogance, prejudice, ignorance, and duplicity as enemies of leadership.
- Call colleagues to responsibility and do not shield them from the growth potential in conflict and adversity.
- Accent an interrogatory style, learning to frame and deploy good questions.

- Value conviction and courage more important than perfection.
- Honor faculty and staff as those giving first voice and meaning to our institutions.
- Understand the complex and tensioned mission of colleges and universities and their governance arrangements.
- Receive criticism of the collegiate enterprise as evidence of our success in educating men and women of critical disposition and as a basis for improving performance and accountability.
- Measure leadership effectiveness in long term goal achievement, in the development of colleagues, and in the long term begrudging respect of those with whom we may work.
- Respect honest dissent and do not demonize those who tender the gift of candor and thereby keep us in touch with the truth of our organizations.
- Exhibit humility but resist those assaults that can wear away the beautiful edges of personality.
- Look behind every leadership arrival to discover what detours and defeats marked the leadership journey.
- Know that leadership promise and performance may be more imperiled by the abandonment of our integrity than by absence of skill and knowledge.
- Walk slowly, listen patiently, and look behind the quiet smile of those within the circle of our care so that we may see what battles of conscience and challenge may contend there.
- Salute in value and practice the power of "servant" and "designer" as informing metaphors of leadership role.
- Hold high expectations for the promise and performance of every talent entrusted to your care but do not confine or imprison the promise of another with narrow expectations.
- Consider the role metaphor of constructive pessimist as a posture that affirms noble motives but keeps us alert to dark and selfish motives among a few.
- Conceptualize leadership as an art form that builds on knowledge derived from theory/research and from action/practice.
- Exemplify civility and respect the dignity of everyone without regard to status or position.
- Retreat not into the womb of ethical neutrality and irresponsibility when moral dilemma stresses mind and heart, but face squarely the call of honor and justice.
- Master both persuasive and coercive sources of authority and learn the moments for effective deployment of each form of authority.
- View politics as the art of being personal and of cultivating influence.
- Embrace determination and persistence as powerful but underrated leadership virtues.

## THE POWER OF ONE

In 1989, Bruce Courtenay published a novel entitled *The Power of One*.[4] Placed in South Africa, in years just preceding, during, and following World War II, the novel chronicled the life of a young English boy caught in the apartheid society of South Africa where Boers had little or no love for Englishmen or Africans, or "Kaffirs" as blacks were called.

Sent off to a Boer school, he was subjected to a series of indignities by his

Boer classmates but learned over the years to be a champion boxer, a skill earning him respect among both Boers and Africans. The novel carries both love and tragedy as PeeKay, the nick name for the primary figure of the novel, develops friendships with a physician and blacks, and works to overcome the demeaning effects of prejudice in South African society. A young woman whom PeeKay loves is killed in a tragic attack on a school they are operating to educate black men and women.

The title of the book, and of the movie made from the novel, is a double entendre. This work of fiction celebrates first the power of one individual life, a life exemplifying persistence and devoted to noble purpose. There is, however, another "power of one," and that is captured in this quote from the movie's ending: "Changes can come from the power of many, but only when the many come together to form that which is invincible—the power of one."

As I noted earlier in these essays, we have many examples of "leadership by the numbers": five practices, seven habits, fourteen rules, twenty-one laws, etc. To those numbers, I have now added some two dozen summary reflections. The numbers are without meaning and the concepts will carry no meaning until the ideas, the values, and the skills carried there are internalized.

I have no hope or expectation that collegiate leaders will memorize my list or the list of anyone else. Ideas, skills, and values are realized in action! I do have the hope that the leadership legacy moments found in these essays and in these summary reflections will prove of stimulus value in having collegiate leaders think about the special and precious role of the institutions they hold in trust and about their role and responsibility in doing so.

Those men and woman who came into collegiate leadership when I did experienced the exhilaration of the baby boom years of the 1960s, the extraordinary growth in both state and federal financial support of higher education. Some wag has noted that the true test of leadership is that the leader could be dead in office for a year and folks out in the organization would not know. I have never been inclined to test that proposition, but there may be some truth there. It is possible that leaders of that day might have been dead in office for a year; and enrollments and finances would have still grown, so great was the enrollment pressure and so pleasant the public financial support.

Not necessarily so for the coming years, however. The leadership issues and challenges facing higher education in America in the opening of the 21st century are not for the uncaring, the unimaginative, the incompetent, the timid, or the arrogant. College leaders are trustees of an organization whose outcomes are damaging and tragic when done without care, competence, and conscience. To carry our students and our faculty/staff in harm's way because we do not know or do not care is an act more to be feared than a bungled surgery. Our mistakes may not bleed. Instead, they will carry hidden scars whose mean and tragic consequence may not be seen until years have passed and remedy is painful or impossible.

There is indeed a "power of one." Just one collegiate leader seduced by pay, power, or prestige, just one collegiate leader neglecting the promise of those who give life to our colleges and universities is one too many. A college leader who designs effective work climates for faculty and staff and who inspires with his or her own personal integrity and curiosity is one to be treasured.

## A SUSTAINING CURIOSITY, A SEARCH FOR MEANING

In the summer of 2006, as I was bringing these essay reflections to close in initial form, I had two pleasant opportunities. The first of these was an invitation to attend the United States Army War College's National Security Seminar at Carlisle Barracks in Pennsylvania. Each day of the seminar the officers and civilians were treated to presentations by leading and provocative minds on strategic issues facing the nation and world. London Financial Times writer Martin Wolf spoke on his 2004 book *Why Globalization Works*,[5] Harvard Kennedy Center scholar Samantha Power spoke on her 2002 book *A Problem from Hell: America and the Age of Genocide*;[6] and we had seminar discussion on Thomas Barnett's 2004 book *The Pentagon's New Map*.[7]

I had never thought of myself as a professional isolated from the flow of world events and ideas, but I returned from this one-week seminar feeling as though I had been living with the mushrooms, shadowed in partial darkness from important intellectual exposure. I brought home copies of the three books named above and three additional volumes, Robert Wright's 2000 book *Nonzero: The Logic of Human Destiny*,[8] Ray Kurzweil's 2005 volume *The Singularity is Near*,[9] and Fareed Zakaria's 2003 book *The Future of Freedom*.[10]

Following this venture with the Army War College, in the later part of the summer, my wife and I enjoyed a wonderful week of vacation at Hilton Head Island, where we went on our honeymoon in 1978 and have returned each summer now for almost thirty years. I can still manage a ten-mile bike ride each morning but spend the afternoons on the ocean-side balcony snacking, napping, and reading. Here was a chance to finish up my reading from the War College Seminar and to wander down to Barnes and Noble. Browsing in the stacks there, I came across a 1998 book by Robert Greene entitled *The 48 Laws of Power*.[11] Back to the numbers again.

Now I haven't finished this book, but I did buy a copy because the Table of Contents was so arresting. Here are a few of the 48 laws:

Law 3: Conceal Your Intentions
Law 6: Court Attention At All Costs
Law 8: Make Others Come toYou—Use Bait If Necessary
Law 11: Learn To Keep People Dependent On You
Law 17: Keep Others in Suspended Terror: Cultivate An Air of Unpredictability
Law 20: Do Not Commit To Anyone
Law 34: Be Royal in Your Own Fashion: Act Like a King To Be Treated Like One

At first glance, these selected tidbits of advice would appear to be in serious counterpoint to all that I have been sharing in these essays. I am therefore anxious to discern what argument and reasoning, what value commitments may serve as foundation for these "48 Laws of Power." I doubt that I would discover this from reading Greene's book, but I am sure I would like to learn whether Robert Greene would enjoy being on the receiving end of his own advice on power!

The contribution of these two professional and personal ventures, however, lies beyond the ideas engaged and resides also in the importance of college leaders cultivating a compulsive and sustaining curiosity. How can we lead an enterprise whose work is to equip and energize curiosity without exemplifying that in our own lives? How can we lead others to the joy of learning without that excitement in our own lives? How can we celebrate the grand journey of advancing on truth without continuing discovery in our own lives?

The one theme that emerged in more than one of the informing volumes I read in the summer of 2006 centered on man's pursuit of meaning in life. Much earlier in my career I had read psychiatrist Victor Frankl's work *Man's Search for Meaning*.[12] Frankl claims in a preface to a 1983 edition, and its seventy-third printing, that he wrote the book in nine days in 1949 and has always been surprised at the book's continued attraction. The book is a narrative of Frankl's experience in World War II Nazi concentration camps. Two of the premier themes are that man's search for meaning is a primary motivation in life and that meaning can be found in moments of suffering. In my administrative and teaching career, I have often suggested to colleagues and students that no one should count themselves an educated person unless they had read this little volume. Parenthetically, two other small books in my short pantheon of works to be read by an "educated" person include two books mentioned earlier in these essays, John Gardner's *Excellence* and Saul Alinsky's *Rules for Radicals*.

Business executive and economics scholar Charles Handy wrote in his 1998 book *The Hungry Spirit* that the lesser hunger in our life is for those things that sustain life but the greater hunger is the search for meaning.[13] His observation is that capitalistic societies behave as though satisfying the lesser hunger will satisfy the greater hunger, only to discover the error of this belief as our lives mature and/or we face a moment of suffering, which is central to the work of Frankl just mentioned. And in his book *NonZero*, previously cited in this chapter, Robert Wright comments that our material and technological progress tends to encourage our seeing life as devoid of meaning.

And so one might argue that not only are our colleges in the business of cultivating curiosity, they are in the business of leading our students to the premier and not inconsequential question of what brings meaning to their lives. Years ago, Bertrand Russell offered this provoking reflection:

> Men who boast of being what is called "practical" are for the most part exclusively preoccupied with means. But theirs is only one half of wisdom. When we take account of the other half, which is concerned with ends, the economic process and the whole of human life take on an entirely new aspect. We ask no longer: What have the producers produced and what has consumption enabled the consumers in their turn to produce? We ask instead: What has there been in the lives of consumers and producers to make them glad to be alive?[14]

How can we lead an enterprise with these purposes without having taken the journey of meaning in our own lives?

There is a legacy to all leadership. One version of that leadership legacy will be carried in the public press. Another will be carried in the minds and hearts of those whose promise we held in trust. An important record of that legacy, however, will be carried in the friendship of our own conscience. May the legacy of our leadership salute the nobility of college and university purpose and the dignity and promise of those who carry our colleges and universities to the future.

## NOTES

1. Andre'Bernard, (ed.). *Rotten Rejections* (Wainscott, NY: Pushcart Press, 2004).

2. E. Grady Bogue, "A Friend of Mine," *Vital Speeches of the Day* 54, no. 20 (August 1, 1988), 615–16.

3. Alan Paton, "The Challenge of Fear," in *What I have learned*, ed. Norman Cousins, 257 (New York, NY: Simon and Schuster, 1966).

4. Bruce Courtenay, *The Power of One* (New York, NY: Random House. 1989).

5. Martin Wolf, *Why Globalization Works* (New Haven, CT: Yale University Press, 2004).

6. Samantha Power, *"A Problem from Hell": American and the Age of Genocide* (New York, NY: Harper Perennial, 2002).

7. Thomas Barnett, *The Pentagon's New Map* (New York, NY: Berkley Books, 2004).

8. Robert Wright, *Nonzero: The Logic of Human Destiny* (New York, NY: Viking, 2000).

9. Ray Kurzwell, *The Singularity Is Near* (New York, NY: Viking 2005).

10. Fareed Zakaria, *The Future of Freedom* (New York, NY: Norton and Company, 2003).

11. Robert Greene, *The 48 Laws of Power* (New York, NY: Viking, 1998).

12. Victor Frankl, *Man's Search for Meaning* (Boston, MA: Beacon Press, 1959).

13. Charles Handy, *The Hungry Spirit* (New York, NY: Broadway Books, 1998).

14. Bertrand Russell, *Authority and the Individual* (New York, NY: Simon and Schuster, 1949), 72–73.

# INDEX

# ABOUT THE AUTHOR

E. Grady Bogue is Professor of Higher Education Administration at the University of Tennessee. He served for eleven years as chancellor of Louisiana State University in Shreveport (1980–91) and for one year as interim chancellor of Louisiana State University in Baton Rouge. He was named chancellor emeritus of LSU Shreveport by the LSU Board of Supervisors in 1991. He received a BS degree in Mathematics (1957), an MS degree (1965) and an EdD (1968) from the University of Memphis and was honored as a distinguished alumnus of the University of Memphis in 1986.

For six years he served as the chief academic officer for the Tennessee Higher Education Commission and prior to that appointment was Assistant Vice President for Academic Affairs at the University of Memphis. He was an instructor of physics with the U.S. Navy from 1961 to 1964, and served as a communications electronics officer with the U.S. Air Force from 1958 to 1961.

Dr. Bogue has authored eight previous books. Four of his latest books are *Quality and Accountability in Higher Education* (Praeger Publishers, 2003), *100 Classic Books in American Higher Education* (Phi Delta Kappa, 2002), *Exploring the Heritage of American Higher Education* (ACE/Oyrx, 2000), and *Leadership by Design* (Jossey-Bass Publishers, 1994). He has published journal pieces in the *Harvard Business Review*, *Leader to Leader*, *Journal of Higher Education*, *Educational Record*, *Phi Delta Kappan*, *Planning for Higher Education*, and *Trusteeship*. Six of his public speeches have been carried in *Vital Speeches of the Day*. He has written periodic columns "On Leadership" for the Nashville and Knoxville, Tennessee Business Journals.

He has been a consultant on planning and evaluation, assessment and accreditation, and leadership and governance to a wide range of colleges and universities, state level agencies, and corporations. He was an American Council Fellow on academic administration in 1974–75, a visiting scholar with the Educational Testing Service in 1988–89, and a consulting scholar with Lipscomb University from 2001 to 2005. He has participated in exchange travel and lectures in China, France, Germany, and republics in the former Soviet Union, and has delivered papers at international meetings in France and Hungary.